Successful Teaching

for Everyone

By Will Fastiggi

Technology for Learners

www.technologyforlearners.com

Copyright © 2019 by Will Fastiggi

ISBN: 9781087264561

CONTENTS

Education is improving the lives of others and for leaving your community and world better than you found it.

- Marian Wright Edelman

PREFACE

Whichever part(s) of this book you read, I hope that you will find the content both helpful and insightful. Everything written here is born from my own teaching journey based on real school experiences and backed by research. All that being said, my drive to write this book comes more from my experience at the receiving end of education as a learner.

Ironically, for the most part, my childhood experience of education was actually quite limited. I was labelled early on as Special Educational Needs (SEN) and went through my entire primary education on the Learning Support register. Upon entering secondary education, I could barely string a sentence together. My maths skills were even further behind. I did not have dyslexia, dyscalculia or ADHD; I was just a slow learner and late bloomer. I was not even particularly good at or fond of sports which remains true to this day.

One redeeming gift that I did have was a penchant for art. I would spend hours drawing and sketching. Towards the end of my primary education that is all I would do, and I had quite a reputation for it too. My class teacher at the time, her hands full with 30 or so other children, would just leave me be. Oftentimes, while the other children were having an English lesson, doing science or solving maths problems, I would be allowed to work alone on my drawings and sketches – either at some quiet corner of the classroom or outside in the playground. To be fair, I was quite happy with this arrangement as well.

There was probably a myriad of reasons why I did not make much academic progress in those early days: apathetic and dispirited teachers, childhood anxiety, bullying, glue ear, socio-economic. In spite of these early challenges (or perhaps because of them), I did develop a certain zeal for education that led me to academic achievements such as First-class honours as well as Distinction for my MA. I mention these achievements not to impress anyone, but rather to impress upon the reader that significant progress, however dire the circumstances appear to be, is possible.

Those honours are in part due to the many dedicated, patient and tenacious teachers who made all the difference for me, personally. The success of these individuals as teachers had nothing to do with the curriculum, school policy or the latest educational mandate. Instead, it had everything to do with their grit and passion. Thanks to successful teaching, I was inspired to be my best and do my best. Later on, I was even inspired to teach!

The fact is, successful teaching changes lives. It certainly changed mine. Just like our students, I believe that we can instinctively recognise what successful teaching looks and feels like. All I have done with this book is to take what we recognise about successful teaching and make it explicit, drawing on my experiences and observations of what works whilst making links to the research findings.

The core ideas and principles in this book build on and draw from extensive research in fields such as assessment, behavioural psychology, cognitive science, economics, history, pedagogy, sociology as well as observations of outstanding teaching practice. Moreover, readers of this book have, it is safe to assume, spent more than a decade in school. Please therefore test all the claims that I make about successful teaching against your experiences as a learner. As there is so much that goes into successful teaching, and so many perspectives to consider, I wholeheartedly invite anyone to critique this book and come forward with their own thoughts for improvement.

This book is not a panacea for all the frustrations and woes that can be associated with teaching. Nevertheless, you can expect to find in this book some answers, inspiration, and I hope, ideas, to help ensure that successful teaching happens for everyone.

Please feel free to email me for more information.

Will Fastiggi

wfastiggi@hotmail.com

ACKNOWLEDGEMENTS

I am tremendously grateful to have worked with many exceptional and highly successful educators, including learning assistants, teachers, educational psychologists and educational leaders. My biggest appreciation goes to the students themselves (and in some cases, the parents) from whom I have learnt and continue to learn so much.

Lastly, I would like to say a big thanks to three teachers in particular, for being willing to share their lessons: Fran, Mariana and Rosangela.

ABOUT THE AUTHOR

Will Fastiggi started his teaching career as a classroom teacher in a large inner-city London school. After more than a decade of teaching, Will has worked in schools in the UK, China, Guatemala, El Salvador, and most recently, Brazil.

Graduating with a Masters in Digital Technologies, Communication & Education from the University of Manchester, Will has worked as a teacher, trainer and ICT Coordinator. As well as having a keen interest in making practical use of digital technologies for schools, Will is especially passionate about working to develop the socio-emotional growth of all learners.

Currently, Will works as Upper Primary Coordinator at The British School, Rio de Janeiro. You can find out more about Will from his blog, technologyforlearners.com.

INTRODUCTION

Successful Teaching matters immensely – it is the single most important factor that determines how students will learn in school. Research consistently shows, for example, that teaching quality, which depends upon the knowledge, skills and dispositions of teachers, is one of the most powerful determinants of student learning (Slater et al., 2012). Moving a child from an average to a top teacher's class could mean that they will learn in six months what would otherwise have taken twelve (Wiliam, 2016). Furthermore, effective teachers help to significantly close the gap on attainment for students from disadvantaged homes (Hamre & Pianta, 2005).

The outcomes from successful teaching are clear. When students are taught successfully, they learn more. By learning more, students go on to make more money, enjoy better health and live longer. For society, successful teaching leads to lower health care costs, lower levels of criminality and increased economic growth (Wiliam, 2018, pp. 9). As there are so many benefits from successful teaching that can be measured and tracked statistically, leaders from around the world have cited quality education as one of their top priorities more frequently than any other sustainable development goal. Anyone who has ever been the recipient of successful teaching will of course realise a multitude of other gains, including personal satisfaction, intellectual stimulation and transferable skills, to name a few.

By virtue of all the real and positive differences that can be made through teaching successfully, this can be a rewarding and noble profession. Teaching, however, is no picnic. Perhaps due in large part to the job's ingrained responsibilities and its potential to make such huge impacts on the lives of young people, successful teaching requires the development and mastery of a great range of qualities. At a minimum, these include self-awareness, dedication, resilience and passion as well as the interpersonal and practical skills associated with classroom management and pedagogy. Evidence shows that the most dramatic gains occur in the first three years of a career, but that teachers continue to improve throughout their careers especially if they engage in professional development (Kini & Podolsky, 2016).

Unfortunately, in the time that it takes to develop the full range of qualities needed, many teachers quit. Approximately 40 per cent, of those who train to become teachers will leave the profession within five years in England (Allen & Sims, 2018, pp. 28). According to Julian Stanley, CEO of Education Support, workload, school culture and student behaviour are amongst the biggest challenges for teachers (Kell, 2018, pp. 12). Having worked in schools across Asia, Europe and Latin America, I have found that teachers everywhere share these same challenges and frustrations – none of which, however, are insurmountable. In fact, with the right support and coaching, most issues are resolvable. Sadly, for the majority of teachers who struggle and consider leaving, the support they need is clearly missing.

The many thousands of teachers who leave the profession yearly is a predictable consequence of what happens when they do not get the support they need. After all, nobody goes through the many years of study and intense training, only to do a lousy job. Ask any teacher, and they will tell you they want to teach successfully and make a positive impact on the lives of the students they teach. Obviously, for those who feel they are consistently not teaching successfully, the work can feel meaningless and the option to leave understandable.

Lest I be misinterpreted, this book is not about criticising any of our current education systems or policies governing these systems. There are many books out there that criticise education or implicitly suggest how money should be spent differently within education, to maximise the return for learners and society at large. Whilst such arguments might be justified, this book goes beyond educational policy, restrictions of school curricula or anything else that the individual educator might take issue with that cannot easily be changed. Instead, all of the ideas and principles covered in this book can be implemented autonomously by teachers irrespective of what schools or politicians prioritise.

The central focus of this book is to distil the field-tested attitudes, behaviours, and where relevant, suggestions for appropriate educational resources, in order to cultivate successful teaching. I have attempted to provide the reader with key ideas and principles that are as broadly applicable as possible to all teaching contexts – information which should be as useful to the kindergarten teacher as it is to the university professor.

Relevant for all stages of teaching and learning, *Successful Teaching for Everyone* has been designed as a guide for educational support staff, teachers and leaders, at all levels of experience, who work in education. It has also been written to both encourage and offer insights for those who might consider entering this profession. Teacher trainees and novice teachers too, will find plenty of invaluable advice, recommendations and research upon which to draw. Likewise, this book can be useful for parents, particularly those who are actively involved in their children's education.

Many of those who are involved in education are busy people and research is often regarded as either too theoretical or otherwise inaccessible. I have therefore done my best to make this book both easily accessible and practical. Each chapter is as self-contained as possible, designed to be interesting to read while providing a toolkit of practical advice and strategies in which successful teaching can be cultivated. Every main section also ends with a summary of the key points. As a result, the book can either be read from beginning to end, or you can simply go directly to the section that you feel is most relevant for you.

Successful Teaching for Everyone is divided into four parts. The first part sets the scene, providing a brief overview of the history of teaching and unpicks some of the most common misconceptions about successful teaching. The remaining three parts accord with the three distinct aspects of successful teaching: managing emotions, teaching strategy and educational resources.

Part One   A Whistle-Stop Tour…

In order to better understand teaching as it is today, Part One gives a whistle-stop tour of the history of teaching – specifically key factors that have shaped teaching over time. Using the history of teaching as a context, some of the most dubious assumptions about what constitutes successful teaching are addressed.

Part Two   Managing Emotions

The topic of values is considered as a prerequisite for meaningful human connection and learning. The fundamental importance of effective behaviour management techniques is then explored as well as defining principles for teachers to keep themselves and students fully engaged. Managing one's own emotions is a recurring theme in this section, which is linked to growth mindset and mindfulness. The usefulness of high-quality feedback for teachers is discussed, and lesson observation tips are given. You will learn how to lead teaching and learning in a school whilst shaping school culture and promoting core values.

Part Three   Teaching Strategy

This part begins with an overview of practical applications for Bloom's taxonomy before drawing on John Hattie's research and evidence-based teaching, to pull out only the most successful teaching strategies. In particular, proven ideas and resources for formative assessment are shared. A case-study on the teaching of mathematics is provided as well as more general approaches to teaching as a whole such as BYOD (Bring Your Own Device), flipped learning and Genius Hour. This section ends by looking at the future of education and the importance of developing an education that incorporates digital citizenship and news literacy.

Part Four   Educational Resources

This final part begins by looking at what is meant by appropriate educational resourcing and why not all educational resources facilitate successful teaching. The role that digital technology has to play is explored and specific examples and recommendations of different technologies are provided. Lastly, recent trends in this area are discussed, including STEAM (Science, Technology, Engineering, Art & Maths) and Makerspaces.

PART ONE

A Whistle-Stop Tour...

1. The History of Teaching

I have never let my schooling interfere with my education.
- **Mark Twain**

In modern usage, teaching is usually approached as the activity delivered by a school teacher. Historically speaking, however, schools are a relatively new phenomenon, and simply listing the duties of teachers does not give an adequate definition of their practice. I therefore propose a succinct definition for teaching that has remained true since the beginning of our species – *teaching is a process for facilitating learning.* As its ultimate purpose is to prepare each generation to function and perform duties in the world, teaching – and the dubious assumptions which accompany it – can only begin to make sense when viewed from a historical perspective.

Unlike other species, humans have always had the ability to organise, store and transmit knowledge via sounds and language. Prior to the advent of technology, oral communication was the only type of teaching that existed. From hunter-gatherer communities to the invention of agriculture 10,000 years ago, people depended on oral communication to acquire knowledge of the plants, animals and land around them. As speech was the primary means by which people passed on learning, this made accurate memorisation a critical skill.

Some forms of knowledge were no doubt expressed through stories, legends, folklore, rituals, and songs. Settlement and trade specialisation amalgamated greater knowledge and skills with each succeeding generation. As communities grew into the first civilizations, those with specialised knowledge taught what they knew to the next generation. The learning process was elaborated and refined through apprenticeships, observation and imitation, all helped along by the spoken word.

Although not widely distributed to the masses at the time, the earliest form of writing appeared with the beginning of the first civilizations around 3,500 BC (Roberts, 2013, pp. 53). In fact, the first examples of educational technology were writing tools. Over thousands of years and across the continents, various surfaces have been used as a medium for writing, including wax-covered writing boards (by the Romans), clay tablets (in the Middle East), strips of bark (in Indonesia, Tibet and the Americas), thick palm-like leaves (in South East Asia) and animal skin parchment (common across the ancient world)[1]. It seems clear that writing was first used, in most cases, to address practical needs such as those of accountancy and administration (Marrou, 1956, pp. 15).

Our understanding of teaching, as it exists within a school system, can be traced to 4th century ancient Greece. Interestingly, the word 'school' actually comes from the Greek 'schole', which means leisure, and, to be sure, schools were available only to the aristocracy, who viewed learning as a form of intellectual leisure. Elsewhere in the ancient world, prominent examples of formal education were evident in the Middle East, China and India, whose systems of education emphasised reading, writing and mathematics (Thomason, 2005, Hardy & Kinney, 2005 & Gupta, 2007).

The diversity of teaching in ancient Greece is notable. It was the Greeks who first created what we would now call primary and secondary schools. They put great emphasis on physical education, considered necessary for improving one's appearance, preparing for war, and retaining good health into old age (Plutarch, 1927). Roman schooling broadly followed the Greek model. Privileged boys attended small schools where they learned grammar and went on to rhetoric school to prepare them for public life (Thomas, 2013, pp. 6).

It is relevant to mention that ancient Greek society effectively had two types of teachers: pedagogues and subject teachers. Pedagogues were trusted members of rich households who accompanied and oversaw the conduct of their masters' sons, sitting beside them while they were being schooled by the subject teachers (Young, 1987). The first pedagogues were actually illiterate slaves (Yannicopoulos, 1985, pp. 173) charged exclusively with pastoral care. By appointing a pedagogue, parents could focus on the more pressing affairs of the household and state. In modern times of course, pastoral duties have been absorbed into the wider role of teachers, which will be discussed further in Part Two.

After the fall of the Roman empire, from about the 8th century, teaching became the responsibility of the religious establishment. Consequently, the knowledge communicated was mostly religious and ethical, and the ultimate purpose of teaching was good conduct (Compayré, 1886). By the end of the Middle Ages, schools would become commonplace in towns and villages across Europe, with the main intention of ensuring children could read and write (Gray, 2008). By Shakespeare's time schools had more or

---

[1] The Division of Rare & Manuscript Collections at the Cornell University Library (2019) provides a repository of these examples for the varied writing surfaces used throughout history.

less become the education system we recognise today.

Across the ancient and medieval world, it was generally only privileged boys who learned to read and write. Girls were taught domestic activities, for example 'to spin, to weave, to prepare food for the table, to superintend the household, and also to sing and to dance' (Compayré, 1886, pp. 15). Boys, by contrast, would be expected to learn academic knowledge and skills, to prepare them to work outside the home. This state of affairs was a reflection of the prevalent attitudes toward gender of the time.

As early as the 6th century, there were institutions of higher education, Catholic and monastic schools in which monks and nuns taught classes (Riché, 1978, pp. 127). These institutions were the forerunners to the first universities founded in Bologna, Paris and Oxford in the 11th and 12th centuries. The emergence of universities spread throughout medieval Europe. Similar to today, this reflected a recognition from political and civic leaders of the value of scholarly expertise to tackle the difficult problems facing society (Grendler, 2004, pp. 2).

Prompted by the German Protestant Reformation, it was during the latter part of the medieval period that the first attempts to make education compulsory for boys and girls emerged (Geister et al., 2006, pp. 145). However, such initiatives did not become widespread until the late 19th century, when governments enacted compulsory attendance laws initially in Europe before gradually spreading to the rest of the world (Soysal et al. 1989).

From the Middle Ages until the latter half of the 20th century, compulsory education was primarily focused on curriculum delivery rather than the needs of the individual learner (Aubrey & Riley, 2016, pp. 7). Schools were in many ways analogous to the factories that drove the Industrial Revolution, characterized by top-down management, standardization and efficiency, with a focus on producing results. As paper and printing were expensive resources during this period, compulsory education in most cases involved no more than rote learning and memorisation – especially in literacy and numeracy.

Interestingly, the systematic and institutional study of education as an academic field started quite late. Teacher education, i.e. the training to help teachers develop effective teaching strategies to use in the classroom, did not begin until the early 19th century. Up until that point, in most cases, it was not even necessary for teachers to have qualifications. As long as one could read, write, spell and was considered to have a positive moral character, he or she was deemed qualified to be a teacher (Ornstein & Levine, 2004).

The 20th century saw sweeping changes, in areas such as politics, science and technology, which significantly impacted education. This was a particularly important time for education in terms of establishing teaching as a discreet process that could be instructed and professionally developed. At the beginning of the 20th century for example, small departments of pedagogy expanded into undergraduate and graduate schools of education. Incidentally, the term 'pedagogy', which is the bedrock for much of this book, has mainly been used since this period as a catch-all term to describe the theories about how learners learn and the resulting methods to be adopted in order to facilitate this learning. Later still, in the second half of the 20th century, Bloom's taxonomy became widespread as a framework in which to codify educational objectives, develop curricula and guide lessons. As Ravitch (2003) notes, educationists sought to create an education profession, which had its own technical language and its own preparation programs towards certification.

At around the same time period, the ideas of philosophers like John Dewey (1859 - 1952) had started to gain ground, and his ideas deserve special mention. Dewey was a U.S. born philosopher who believed strongly that education should focus on practical life experience and social interactions rather than the more traditional instruction and rote learning widely practised until the early 20th century. In particular, Dewey promoted the idea of "learning by doing" rather than learning as a passive experience. His ideas caused considerable controversy at the time, but they laid the foundation for progressive education which strongly informs the constructivist approach we see across curricula today. Put simply, constructivism is the theory that people construct their knowledge and understanding of the world through experience and reflection on that experience as opposed to passively receiving information.

Although Dewey did not use the term 'constructivism', his point of view can be considered constructivist. Dewey argued, for example, that teachers have an important responsibility in facilitating learning by encouraging and channelling individuals' curiosity and motivation so they can develop intellectually (Aubrey & Riley, 2016, pp. 7). He also argued that a curriculum could only work if it related to the activities and responsibilities that students will likely have after leaving school. According to Dewey, schools should be concerned with the education of the whole child, including the intellectual, social, physical, and emotional needs of each student.

Advancing this sentiment, Dewey believed that the role of teachers was multifaceted. In his view, teachers should facilitate a stimulating learning environment while helping students develop transferable skills to thrive and contribute to a democratic society. This type of pedagogy is known as learner-centred and is intended to enable learners to engage with learning while preparing them to become active members of their communities and society. It is these core ideas from Dewey that have persisted and continue to be the bedrock of educational practice today.

Still, Dewey's conclusions, compelling as they may sound, are more grounded in ideology than in reliable data. Considering the history of education, it is unsurprising that educational policy today is so contentious. The act of teaching, as a form of educational enquiry, is not viewed as a disciplined form of knowledge. Unlike other fields, education never began with commonly agreed upon canons of thought about its subject matter or effective practice to guide teachers. Education, more than any other field of study in fact, continues to be an area in which new ideas routinely emerge that have not been carefully scrutinised much less viewed through the lens of empirical analysis:

...both law and medicine have well established, research-based standards and procedures. In law, there is a body of case law and commonly accepted procedures that future lawyers must master. In medicine, there are standard tests, standard diagnoses, and standard treatments for known ailments that future doctors must master. This is not the case in education, where pedagogues have debated what to teach, how to teach, how to test, whether to test, and which research methods are acceptable. Because of this lack of consensus on even the most elementary procedures, teachers have received a constant din of conflicting signals from the leaders of the field. In the past, dubious research findings grounded more in ideology than in data were given credibility by pedagogical leaders (Ravitch, 2003).

Moreover, unlike the medical profession, in which advances generally result in better health outcomes for the population, and doctors need to keep abreast of the latest research in their field, the same is not widely true of the teaching profession. Reflecting on my own training and induction into teaching, for example, I was never taught educational theory or even expected to stay versed in the latest in educational research. Virtually everything I have learned about educational theory has been prompted by my own curiosity and enquiry rather than any professional expectation.

This reflects yet another area of contention within the educational community. Even today, it is still not agreed among educators themselves, whether teaching is a craft best taught by example or a profession with a coherent theory at its core. In my opinion, teaching, if it is to be successful, should be considered both a craft and a profession. Certainly, if teaching was only a craft that could be imitated, there would be little point of this book. I also agree with those who refer to teaching as a vocation, or a calling to make a positive difference to the lives of students – a point I will expand on in Part Two.

The only fact that is commonly agreed about teaching is that it has always been a necessity. As we have seen, the aims, ideals and methods of teaching, are an area of much contention. In the absence of commonly established canons of knowledge regarding what might constitute successful teaching, a number of implicit and explicit assumptions have become widespread. Before looking at what constitutes successful teaching, I begin by uncovering some of the most persistent and dubious assumptions as they pertain specifically to teaching.

This is *not to say* that all of the dubious assumptions I list here are completely unfounded – at least not in all contexts. I do believe, as Daisy Christodoulou (2018) has stressed that it is beneficial for the education of our students, to carefully scrutinise the assumptions in education, by holding them up to the light of common sense and empirical analysis. Duly informed, let's begin.

2. Dubious Assumptions

Assumption 1 – Teachers' subject-matter knowledge is a key determinant of their success in the classroom.

This assumption is more likely to be held by secondary educators because they are content specialists, unlike primary teachers, who are generalists teaching a range of subjects.

As a former Primary ICT Coordinator, a role in which I would regularly assist and observe teachers in their delivery of ICT lessons, I came to identify this assumption as a dubious one. Teachers with no subject knowledge to teach a lesson about programming or spreadsheets, for example, would obviously be unable to deliver their lessons. However, once the teacher had obtained a level of the necessary subject-matter knowledge (to be at least one step ahead of the students), I noticed that the teacher could deliver lessons that were at least as good as – if not better than – the lessons of another teacher who had more in-depth and relevant subject-matter knowledge but lacked the expertise to teach.

Another example of Assumption 1 plays out in the case of guest speakers.

Occasionally, schools invite guest speakers to present to students about a specific topic owing to their expertise in a given field. Unfortunately, I have learnt the hard way that just because someone is an archaeologist, a political theorist, a theologian or a mechanical engineer, does not necessarily mean that they can convey their subject-matter knowledge in a way that students find engaging or can understand. On several occasions, I have seen students completely disengage and phase out after a particularly dry presentation. This had nothing to do with the guest speakers' subject-matter knowledge but everything to do with their ability to grab the students' attention and explain concepts in an age-appropriate manner.

According to John Hattie's (2009) research (which we will look at in more detail later on in Part Three), teacher subject-matter knowledge had an effect size of 0.19, meaning that it was far less effective in terms of influencing student outcomes than other factors like classroom management (0.52) or effective teacher feedback (0.75). This .19 effect size is also well below the hinge point of .40. (Hattie found that to have a positive or negative effect on learning, .40 was the threshold needed for a student to make a year's worth of growth for a year's input.)

As Khwaja (2006) states, the response to ineffective teachers therefore should not necessarily be to send them on professional development courses to enhance their subject knowledge and understanding:

'The effective primary teacher needs to know and understand the child's world in order to help make these connections... The effective teacher must also be able to select teaching methods appropriate for the pupils in his class' (Khwaja, 2006, pp. 18).

There are clearly a wide range of qualities that make for a successful teacher and successful teaching. Indeed, whilst teachers' subject knowledge is *a* factor in successful teaching, there are many other factors involved.

Assumption 2 – All students can hear what you say.

One of the most common implicit yet least talked about dubious assumptions in teaching is that each student can hear what you say. Growing up with a hearing impairment, I know firsthand this assumption is false. I spent many years of my primary education completely oblivious to what the teacher was talking about simply because I could not hear what was being said. I would not have described myself as significantly deaf either (I am somewhere in the range of mild to moderate). However, in the classroom context, with plenty of background noise and a softly-spoken or quick-talking teacher, it would often be a real challenge to catch everything the teacher was saying – and impossible at the back of the hall during an assembly.

Nowadays of course, it is one of the first things that I notice when doing lesson observations. Is the teacher always facing the children when speaking? Is she talking loudly enough and slowly enough to be consistently heard – even for the students at the back of the class? When a student gives an answer to one of the teacher's questions (and does so quietly), does the teacher repeat the answer back, to make sure that everyone has heard what the student has just said? Even if there are no students in the classroom with a registered hearing impairment, one should not assume that students can always hear what is being said. World Health Organisation figures suggest that, worldwide, 15 per cent of adults and 5.3 per cent of children have some degree of hearing loss.

The other obvious implication of this fact is that students should be taught to project their voices. Whenever students are given an opportunity to speak, they should be encouraged to address their audience loudly and clearly – especially, in the case of assemblies or other situations in which the student has to present. As one of the most basic tenets of communication then, speaking clearly and making sure that everyone can hear what you say is low lying fruit for successful teaching.

Assumption 3 – All students can read what you write.

In observing lessons in many schools, I have come across several cases of teachers who have poor handwriting. Sometimes a student might call the teacher out to clarify what has been written – but most of the time students will not bother. In these circumstances, I see the students squinting or turning their head sideways to make out the board. This might sound minor but if it happens regularly enough, it can have serious implications for students' learning. It should go without saying that as educators we are all role-models, and this includes modeling the appropriate presentation of our work. At worst, if a student is unable to read a teacher's feedback comment, or information on the whiteboard, they might miss a key learning opportunity. A teacher's messy handwriting may even serve as a disincentive for students to improve their own handwriting and work presentation.

For the teacher with messy handwriting, this need not be a handicap – as long as the teacher acknowledges and compensates accordingly. For example, as a teacher, I would compensate for my hearing impairment by making sure to move closer to a student who was speaking. In this way, my weakness became a strength; I would take ownership of the classroom space and *always* encourage the student addressing the class to speak clearly.

For the teacher with messy handwriting, there can be a whole range of successful compensatory approaches. As Simmons (2013) writes:

Sometimes I type separate sheets of comments and staple one to each student paper... Sometimes I email the comments... Students have learned to follow up with me in order to decode my comments... However brief, the one-on-one conferences help me build better relationships with students, especially those most terrified of writing... I write little on the board, relying on projections instead. When there is writing to be done, whenever possible, I have students do it, which reinforces the student-driven classroom atmosphere I want to foster.

If the teacher's shortcoming cannot be directly fixed, then it at least should be compensated for. If compensation is generous enough, it can actually improve teaching in unforeseen ways.

Assumption 4 – Student engagement equates to learning.

This is another implicit assumption that I see made in teaching at all levels. On the one hand, I have thankfully observed many lessons in which it is fair to say that students were very engaged. This is unsurprising; as educators, the last thing we want is for learners to be bored, their minds wandering. The best way to hook students into their learning should be a key focus when planning lessons. On the other hand, the ultimate question to ask, independent of engagement, is whether or not new learning is taking place.

As Sheninger (2016, pp. 66) states,

'Having fun, collaborating, communicating, and being creative are all very important elements that should be embedded elements of pedagogically sound lessons, but we must not lose sight of the connection to, and evidence of, learning. Thus, students can walk away from a lesson or activity having been very engaged but with very little form of new knowledge construction, conceptual mastery, or evidence of applied skills.'

I have observed (and delivered) many lessons in which everything was well-prepared, there was plenty of animated discussion and everyone had enjoyed the lesson – but students had learnt nothing new. For example, students playing Minecraft in a maths lesson are generally glued to their screens and working collaboratively to build and explore. How to measure what they actually learn though? Many students certainly learn nothing new about Minecraft, a software they already know how to use well. If the application is not used as a stimulus for their writing or some other clear learning outcome, then there is little point in using it. In this example, the question then comes down to how well the technology is integrated into the lesson – a question we will explore more in Part Four of this book. The main point is that engagement is a necessary condition for learning to take place – but by itself, engagement is not sufficient to guarantee learning. As Tomlinson and McTighe (2006, pp. 28) assert, teachers should avoid activities that are like "cotton candy – pleasant enough in the moment but lacking long-term substance".

Assumption 5 – Play has nothing to do with learning.

Play can be defined as anything we do simply for the joy of doing it rather than as a means to an end. On the surface, play might seem like an unnecessary activity in a context of serious learning. However, recent research proves this false – play has a very important role in student learning.

There are at least four reasons that explain why play is a fuel for learning:

1. According to Stuart Brown (2010), play leads to brain plasticity, adaptability and creativity. As a result, play opens our minds and broadens our perspectives, making us more receptive to the ideas of others.

2. Play is, according to Greg Mckeown (2014), an antidote to stress. In addition to reducing productivity, stress can shut down parts of the brain. Mckeown presents evidence that shows stress increases activity in the area that monitors emotions, the amygdala, while reducing activity in the part responsible for cognitive function, the hippocampus. The result is that we cannot think clearly, which is obviously a barrier to learning. Play, however, can reverse this barrier, by helping to reduce stress.

3. Edward M Hallowell (1994), a psychiatrist who specialises in the science of the brain explains that there is a positive effect of play on what is known as the brain's 'executive function'. This includes planning, prioritising, scheduling, delegating, deciding and analysing.

4. Maria Montessori (1967, pp. 141-142) noted that 'one of the greatest mistakes of our day is to think of movement itself, as something apart from the higher functions… Mental development must be connected with movement and dependent on it.' Increasingly, research shows that physical activity strongly influences cognition through helping to regulate alertness, attention and motivation (e.g., Hillman et al., 2009). As play is often associated with physical movement, it makes sense to promote play

in order to bolster learning.

The ramifications of all this evidence and research into play are significant. We see that, in order to develop cognitive processes, play that fuels positive emotions, reduces stress and promotes physical exercise is a good thing. Golden Time, for example, is a behaviour management strategy used in many primary schools. It is a period of up to an hour, where children stop their usual classwork and spend time immersed in playful activities that are not on offer at other points in the week. Although the behaviour management aspect of Golden Time is contentious (i.e. rewarding children with extra playtime for simply behaving well), the benefits of play for learning should not be underestimated. By providing students of any age with a break from the usual pattern of teaching through play, students can benefit from more learning than would otherwise have been the case.

Assumption 6 – Teacher-led fact-giving should be avoided in favour of allowing students to "discover things for themselves".

There is a general rhetoric in education that states the teacher should be a facilitator for student learning rather than a "sage on the stage" doling out facts. Instead of the teacher transmitting knowledge to students, it is widely considered best teaching practice for students to discover things for themselves. According to Christodoulou (2014), this idea can be traced back to the work of the American psychologist Jerome Bruner in the 1960s. Bruner advocated a pedagogy in which the learner interacts with the material to be learned in the manner of a self-investigator to encourage independent thinking and problem-solving. Inquiry-based learning, problem-based learning and project-based learning have been born from Bruner's work.

There are three assumptions here, which Christodoulou has identified:

1. Concepts are more fully remembered.

2. Learners are more motivated to learn if they have to discover by themselves.

3. By discovering for themselves, learners will be more able to find solutions in new problem situations.

To what extent are each of these assumptions actually true? Although, as I will explain, some degree of discovery learning can be useful, it should not be used in isolation, and it should only be used in certain situations. Let's look at why by interrogating each one of these assumptions:

1. *Are concepts more fully remembered by allowing students to "discover things for*

themselves"?

It depends on learners' previous knowledge. This is because conceptual understanding is only possible by knowing facts – and usually, lots of facts. As Christodoulou (2014, pp. 20) points out, we know that long-term memory is capable of storing thousands of facts, and when these are memorised around a particular topic, these facts form what is called a 'schema'. When we meet new facts about that topic, we assimilate them into that schema – and if we already have a lot of facts in that particular schema, it is much easier for us to learn facts about that topic. To put it another way, factual knowledge makes cognitive processes work better.

Christodoulou's example clarifies this well:

'Critics of fact-learning will often pull out a completely random fact and say something like: who needs to know the date of the Battle of Waterloo? What does it matter? Of course, pulling out one fact like this on its own does seem rather odd. But the aim of fact-learning is not to learn just one fact – it is to learn several hundred, which taken together form a schema that helps you to understand the world. Thus, just learning the date of the Battle of Waterloo will be of limited use. But learning the dates of 150 historical events from 3000 BC to the present day and learning a couple of key facts about why each event was important will be of immense use, because it will form the fundamental chronological schema that is the basis of all historical understanding.' (Christodoulou, 2014, pp. 20)

As Hirsch (2017, pp. 79) states, many teachers now deplore the "memorising" of mere facts. According to this line of thought: "We need less memorisation of facts, and more emphasis on critical thinking skills for the 21st century". Hirsch highlights this fallacy by presenting evidence showing that a mind well-stocked with facts is essential to critical thinking and to looking things up:

'Critical thinking does not exist as an independent skill. Cognitive scientists have shown since the 1940s that human skills are domain specific, and do not transfer readily from one domain to the next. No matter how widely skilled people may be, as soon as they confront unfamiliar content their skill degenerates. An unfamiliar topic will quickly degrade both reading and writing. The domain specificity of skills is one of the most important scientific findings of our era for teachers and parents to know about.' (Hirsch, 2017, pp. 79)

It is true, however, that knowledge must be meaningful. In other words, the goal is not simply to have students know a lot – it is to have them know things in the service of effective thinking. As Willingham (2009, pp. 50) makes clear, teachers should not take the importance of knowledge to mean that they should create lists of facts for students to learn. Simply put, knowledge pays off when the facts are related to one another.

16

Incidentally, the effects of knowledge described is also why it is so important to get children to read. Books expose children to more facts and to a broader vocabulary than any other activity, and persuasive data indicate that people who read for pleasure enjoy cognitive benefits throughout their lifetime (Willingham, 2009, pp. 49).

2. Are learners more motivated to learn if they have to discover by themselves?

Not necessarily. It stands to reason that as long as the subject matter is presented to learners in an engaging way, learners will be just as motivated to learn in a direct-instruction-based lesson as they would be through discovery learning.

There are two more related problems with these first two assumptions about discovery learning, particularly for younger learners and especially in the domain of natural science. The great learning theorist Piaget long ago made clear that younger learners see interpret and understand the world differently from adults and are not capable of carrying out the abstract cognitive transformations necessary for fruitful knowledge construction as it occurs in the sciences (Pedro de Bruyckere et. al, 2015, pp. 50).

Hattie and Yates (2013, pp. 78) add a further problem, closely related to the importance of prior knowledge:

'... several studies have found that low ability students will prefer discovery learning lessons to direct-instruction-based lessons, but learn less from them. Under conditions of low guidance, the knowledge gap between low and high ability students tend to increase. The lack of direct guidance has greater damaging effects on learning in low ability students especially when procedures are unclear, feedback is reduced, and misconceptions remain as problems to be resolved rather than errors to be corrected.'

3. By discovering for themselves, will learners more easily be able to find solutions in new problem situations?

As with critical thinking, problem solving is another all-purpose skill that is proffered a lot in education. According to Hirsch (2017, pp. 84): *'There exists no consistent all-purpose problem-solving skill, independent of domain-specific knowledge.'* There is now plenty of research and evidence to demonstrate that even when people are shown how to solve a problem in one domain, they tend to be baffled by a similar problem in another domain. Learners, especially the younger they are, need active guidance from their teacher through knowledge transmission.

Einstein reportedly said, "Imagination is more important than knowledge." As Willingham (2009, pp. 46) points out though, if Einstein did actually say this, he was wrong: 'Knowledge is more important, because it's a prerequisite for imagination, or at least the sort of imagination that leads to problem solving, decision making, and creativity.' It is clear that the cognitive processes which are most esteemed are intertwined with knowledge.

The pure discovery approach to learning is simply not as effective compared to when students are guided by a teacher to the intended learning outcomes. Even Bruner himself, some years later, replaced the concept of "discovery learning" with "guided discovery". Guided discovery, in which each step of learners' independent enquiry is scaffolded, should go hand in hand with a certain amount of knowledge transmission from the teacher. Problem-based learning, for example, is simply inappropriate for acquiring new knowledge or insights though it could be useful for applying and honing existing skills and for making connections between different concepts.

Pedro de Bruyckere et. al (2015, pp. 51) assert that, as with many other educational initiatives, the effectiveness of discovery learning is dependent on the target group, the objectives and the subjects. For novice learners, pure discovery learning, although it can be something to strive towards, should never be the main method. Experts, on the other hand, possess sophisticated schemas in long-term memory, allowing them to deal differently with problems and solve them in different ways. The more novice the learner is then, the more important support and guidance are, to the point where, for experts in a domain, discovery learning might well be effective.

Assumption 7 – Knowledge and skills are distinct.

Christodoulou makes the case that knowledge and skills are intertwined, and they are intertwined to such an extent that it is impossible to extricate discreet skills and teach them independently. Skill progression depends upon knowledge accumulation. For example, building knowledge by committing facts to memory (e.g., the alphabet), allows learners to improve their communication skills. Likewise, learning a foreign language requires knowledge of vocabulary and grammar. Learning all of the 12 times tables, and learning them all confidently that we do not have to think of the answer when multiplication problem is presented, is the basis of mathematical skill and understanding. Learning to build websites requires knowledge of HTML and CSS. Learning to drive requires knowledge of road signs and conditions. The list of examples goes on and on – basically, all critical thinking processes are tied to background knowledge. In all domains, considerable knowledge is found to be an essential prerequisite to expert skill.

Gibson (1998, pp. 46-47) gives the example of Shakespeare's education, which shows just how closely knowledge and skills are connected:

'Shakespeare's education at Stratford-upon-Avon Grammar School gave him a thorough grounding in the use of language and classical authors. Although his schooling might seem narrow and severe today (schoolboys learned by heart over 100 figures of rhetoric), it proved an excellent resource for the young playwright. Everything Shakespeare learned in school he used in some ways in his plays. Some of his early plays seem to have a very obvious pattern and regular rhythm, almost mechanical and like clockwork. But having mastered the rules, he was able to break and transform them… On this evidence, Shakespeare's education has been seen as an argument for the value of learning by rote, of constant practice, of strict rule-following. Or, to put it another way, 'discovery favours the well-prepared mind'. His dramatic imagination was fueled by what would now be seen as sterile exercises in memorisation and constant practice. What was mechanical became fluid, dramatic language that produced thrilling theatre.'

Clearly, Shakespeare's skill as a playwright came from the way he used knowledge. As Christodoulou (2015, pp. 22) argues, 'a fact-filled education did not stifle Shakespeare's genius; on the contrary, this education allowed that genius to flourish'. The same can be said of the fact-filled education received by many great writers, scientists, policy-makers, economists and inventors who have made enormous positive contributions to the world. In fact, the entire Industrial Revolution was driven by men who had received an education based on rote learning and memorization.

'By assuming that pupils can develop chronological awareness, write creatively or think like a scientist without learning any facts, we are guaranteeing that they will not develop any of those skills' (Christodoulou, 2015, pp. 22).

The idea that teaching strategies for analysing or thinking critically will allow our learners to exercise their skills of analysis or critical thinking is flawed. As Harry Fletcher-Wood (2018, pp. 16) explains, 'we can teach students to think deeply, critically and creatively, but only about what they know.' In other words, knowledge – not skill – is the most critical factor that determines how much students can learn:

'What students know dictates what they can learn. Students with low reading ability but good knowledge of baseball will understand a text about baseball as well as students with high reading ability and a low knowledge of baseball' (Recht and Leslie, 1988).

Assumption 8 – The multiplicity of technology used by teachers in classrooms automatically improves students' learning.

To be sure, technology's effectiveness depends on how it is integrated into teaching and learning. Richard Clark and David Feldon (2005) for example, confirm that the effectiveness of tech-based learning is determined primarily by the way the technological medium is used and by the quality of the instruction accompanying it. It is worth exploring Dr. Ruben Puentedura's SAMR model, a practical framework which shows the impact of technology on teaching and learning. As shown below, his model moves through various stages, beginning at a basic level of learning in the substitution phase through to a level where learning is transformational at the redefinition level.

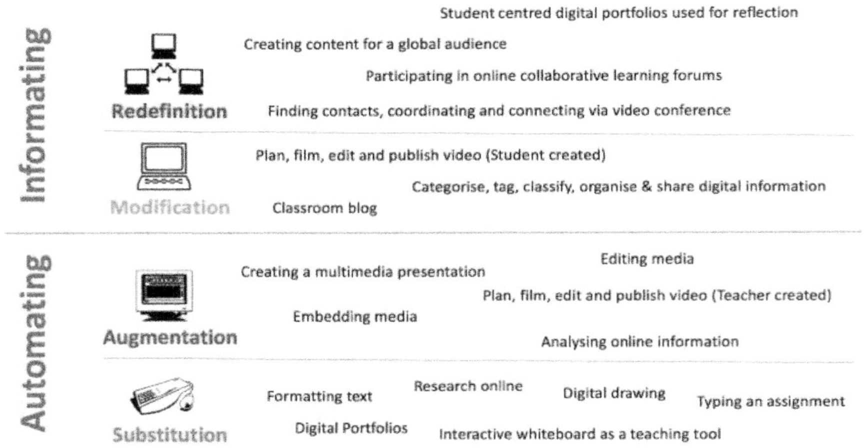

The SAMR model is powerful because it enables us to think about how learning can be extended through the use of technology. The four stages of the SAMR model are summarised here:

Substitution – Technology acts as a direct tool substitute, with no functional change. For example, students may type up notes on a word processor instead of writing by hand in an exercise book.

Augmentation – Technology still acts as a direct tool substitute, but with functional improvements. When typing on a word processor, augmentation means that the learning process can become more efficient and engaging. Images can be added, text can be hyperlinked and edits can be made quickly.

These first two stages of the SAMR model represent enhancements of existing ways of

20

working. Digital technology is not necessary in order to carry out the learning task. The technology simply provides a digital medium for learning to take place, which may enhance learning.

Modification - By this stage technology not only enhances learning, it also significantly transforms it. Consider students starting a blog in which they share their work with a worldwide audience. As the blogs are accessible to a much wider audience, students can feel the need to spend more time refining their written work. In this way, both student learning and literacy improve.

Redefinition - This level requires the teacher to think about learning activities that were previously inconceivable without the use of technology. This could be, for instance, a Google Hangout session that takes place between students from different countries in order for students to swap information about their home countries in real-time. Likewise, the use of Google Docs for students in different parts of the world to collaborate on a shared assignment facilitates learning opportunities that would be impossible without such technology.

The modification and redefinition levels represent transformational stages in terms of student learning, as the technology is actively helping to transform the way in which learning can occur.

The SAMR model is essentially a planning tool that helps to design better learning activities for students. The framework provides pedagogical insight into how technology can and should be used in the classroom. New technology in and of itself will not necessarily improve students' learning outcomes. In order to get the most out of technology for learners, I would make the following recommendations in light of the SAMR model:

1. Always consider whether or not the technology improves the learning process. If the learning process is enhanced through the use of technology, then it's appropriate to use – if not, more traditional methods can work just as well if not better.

2. Collaboration is extremely important, particularly if you are looking at learning from a social constructivist perspective. Consider how you can use technology to facilitate collaboration.

3. Ensure that you use technology to expose students to the outside world. This not only helps to improve their cultural understanding and international-mindedness, it can be great for building key literacy skills.

Assumption 9 – Boys benefit if they have male teachers.

All the evidence available points to the fact that the gender of the teacher has little or no effect on the learning performance of boys in school (Pedro de Bruyckere et. al, 2015, pp. 183). Indeed, having worked as a male teacher for more than a decade, I have never felt that I had any inherent advantage in the classroom.

Contrary to popular belief, boys do not benefit in any measurable way from having a male teacher. This is important to note, since according to statistics from the Department for Education, approximately only one in four teachers are men in England – accounting for 38% of secondary and 15% of primary schools. Using data provided by the World Bank, the figures look similar across Europe and North America; female representation in teaching markedly outweighs the number of men in the profession. Still, there is often media attention given to highlight such figures and attract more men into the profession.

Assumption 10 – Teaching is best delivered in a format that matches students' learning preferences.

This was one of the key things that I had to unlearn from teacher training. First, evidence from Clark (1982) shows that learners who have reported preferring a particular instructional technique typically derive little benefit from experiencing it repeatedly. The second problem deals with the concept of learning styles itself. The assumption that people can be classified into distinct learning types receives little to no support from objective studies. As Pedro de Bruyckere et. al (2015, pp. 21) state:

'Most people do not fit one particular style; the information used to assign people to styles is often inadequate; and there are so many different styles that it becomes cumbersome to link particular learners to particular styles.'

Rohrer and Pashler (2012, pp. 117) found no evidence that children taught in their preferred learning style performed any better than if they were taught through a non-preferred style:

'The contrast between the enormous popularity of the learning style approach and the lack of any credible scientific proof is both remarkable and disturbing'.

It is clear that the learning style theory as it is applied to classroom instruction has been aggressively promoted by those who stand to profit from educational products that promote learning style assessments and resources.

Assumption 11 – Teachers should talk less.

Teacher-led discussion is the most universal of all classroom practices. Since the ideas of John Dewey have gained momentum though, too much teacher talk in classrooms is now widely looked down on for creating a passive learning environment. But how much is too much? Certainly, it stands to reason that students will quickly become disengaged if the teacher is not presenting the material in an interesting way. However, sometimes it can be necessary for teacher talk to dominate the classroom discussion.

There are significant differences among countries in the relative proportions of teacher and student talk. Teachers in the U.S and the UK for example, talk less than teachers in countries with higher average levels of achievement. For example, a 1999 Trends in International Mathematics and Science Study ('TIMSS') video finds that in U.S. middle school mathematics classrooms, there are eight teacher words for every student word. In Japan and Hong Kong, the figures are thirteen and sixteen, respectively (Hiebert et al., 2003). As Dylan William (2018, pp. 90) explains, although many people assume teachers in the US or UK talk too much, they actually talk less than teachers in countries with higher performance. In terms of successful teaching therefore, how much students learn depends much more on what teachers are saying and how they are saying it, rather than how much they are saying.

Assumption 12 – Cognitive performance can be enhanced through "brain training".

In recent years, "brain training" has become big business around the world. Software companies have been quick to develop "brain games" with the promise improving everything from problem-solving skills, hand-eye coordination and memory to a whole range of other cognitive abilities. However, regular practice with these games have not been shown to significantly improve cognitive functioning. In a report in the journal Nature, Adrian Owen of the Cognition and Brain Sciences Unit at Cambridge University and his colleagues conclude: '... regular brain training confers no greater benefit than simply answering general knowledge questions using the Internet'.

Similarly, Pedro de Bruyckere et. al (2015, pp. 110) state:

The word "brain" is misleading since any training necessarily involves the brain. There is as yet no evidence at all that brain training that is aimed at improving general cognitive abilities such as fluid intelligence will in any way be effective.

In October 2014, 73 psychologists, cognitive scientists and neuroscientists from around the world signed an open letter stating that companies marketing "brain games" that are meant to slow or reverse age-related memory decline and enhance other cognitive functions are exploiting customers by making "exaggerated and misleading claims" that are not based on sound scientific evidence.'

The implication for teaching is simple – there is no general training method that can help improve cognitive performance.

Assumption 13 – Your memory is the product of what you want to remember.

Cognitive science shows that your memory is not a product of what you want to remember or what you try to remember; it is a product of what you think about (Willingham, 2009, pp. 53). To teach successfully, teachers must consider what an assignment will actually make their students think about, because that is what they will remember. How can this be achieved in practice though?

As Willingham (2009, pp. 64-65) explains:

'Students often refer to good teachers as those who "make the stuff interesting." It's not that the teacher relates the material to students' interests – rather, the teacher has a way of interacting with students that they find engaging.'

In Part Two, 'Human Connection', this idea of the teacher-student relationship is explored in more depth. For now, suffice to say, a good teacher-student relationship will make it more likely that that students pay attention. Once the teacher has the students' attention, the teacher must deliver the lesson in a coherent way so that students will understand and remember. Several strategies for achieving this will be outlined in Part Three, 'Teaching Strategy'.

Assumption 14 – Homework improves student learning.

Homework has long been a contentious topic in education. According to evidence from Hattie (2009), homework in primary schools shows virtually no effect (0.15), whereas homework in secondary schools shows a significant effect on student learning (0.64). But as Hattie explains emphatically, this does not mean that homework should be eradicated in primary schools:

"If you try and get rid of homework in primary schools many parents judge the quality of the school by the presence of homework. So, don't get rid of it. Treat the zero as saying, "It's probably not making much of a difference but let's improve it". Certainly, I think we get over obsessed with homework. Five to ten minutes has the same effect of one hour to two hours. The worst thing you can do with homework is give kids projects. The best

thing you can do is to reinforce something you've already learnt."

(John Hattie: Homework and Its Value -
https://www.bbc.co.uk/sounds/play/b04dmxwl)

Hattie highlights that some forms of homework have a bigger effect than others. The point is to make sure that homework is meaningful and relevant to what students are learning. Teacher monitoring is also key, especially for younger students, who naturally require more supervised and structured homework activities (rather than homework that is project-based). It can be a challenge for many teachers to find appropriate homework tasks for their students to do, especially at primary school age. Nevertheless, the right homework activity pitched at the right level to reinforce learning and which is closely monitored and includes feedback, can make a significant difference.

It was for this reason that I designed Classroom Flipped (http://classroomflipped.com/), to connect both teachers and students with the most relevant online sources of information and learning activities from digital platforms such as BrainPOP and Discovery Education. The website can make it easier for teachers to set relevant homework activities according to the International Primary Curriculum (IPC). My recommendation is for all schools to have something similar, which enables them to make sure that homework is well-matched to what the curriculum covers. For more information about BrainPOP, take a look at Part Four.

Assumption 15 – Teachers talk about teaching.

Collaborative conversations among teachers about what constitutes successful teaching can make a huge difference, but they are unfortunately quite rare. According to Hattie (2015, pp. 23):

'Yes, we create staffrooms for teachers to work and debate together, but the discussions are typically dominated by curriculum, students and assessments – rarely by learning, and even more rarely by the impact of teaching on student learning. There is almost a conspiracy in saying 'I acknowledge that you teach differently from me, and I respect that', which is code for 'Just leave me alone'.'

In other words, just bringing teachers together does not in itself necessarily improve teaching practice. The topics that teachers discuss generally make no positive difference to their teaching quality.

Furthermore, negative attitudes and conversations can actually be fairly pervasive in teaching. Anyone who works in a school setting will likely be familiar with at least one teacher who seems to complain about everything. Instead of looking for the positives, the default for such jaded teachers is to look for and brood on anything they consider a problem. Such negativity can become contagious and is potentially damaging to school culture, not to mention teaching and learning.

There must be deliberate efforts to both cultivate an overall feeling of positivity and also to facilitate opportunities for teachers to discuss best practice. TeachMeets, for example, in which teachers come together informally, to deliver short presentations to one another on key ideas, can be particularly effective.

Assumption 16 – Streaming makes a difference.

Streaming (also known as tracking or setting) refers to the grouping of students by ability. The rationale for streaming is that it supposedly makes it possible to teach more effectively and allows students to move ahead at a pace in line with their abilities. Meta-analysis studies summarising more than 300 studies of streaming, however, show that streaming has minimal effects on learning (Hattie, 2009). While there can be benefits for higher ability students, streaming tends to have a detrimental impact on students of lower ability. As Oakes et al. (1993, pp. 20) explain:

'Students not in the highest tracks have fewer intellectual challenges, less engaging and supportive classrooms, and fewer well-trained teachers.'

I can certainly affirm from my own experience of having spent so much time in Special Educational Needs (SEN) groups, there was generally very little worthwhile work to do, and I spent a lot of time spent filling in (or more often colouring in) the blanks of worksheets. Teacher expectations in these groups was generally very low, and consequently I learned little. This is not to say that ability groupings do not have a place. For example, I also had the experience, upon entering secondary school, of being in other low sets and making rapid progress – thanks to the determination and passion of the teacher.

Digging further into the qualitative evidence on this, John Hattie (2009, pp. 91) makes an important point:

'It seems that the quality of teaching and the nature of the student interactions are the key issues, rather than the compositional structure of the classes.'

This would explain why Kulik and Kulik (1992) found more benefits for learning from 'within-class ability grouping' and differentiation than what has been found in other research studies on streaming. If you are teaching in a school where there is a policy of streaming, this by itself should not negatively impact the learning of lower ability students. What makes the biggest difference is successful teaching – which will be the focus for the rest of this book.

Before moving on though, it is worth emphasising that for the most part, teachers already do an excellent job of creating challenging lessons. In addition, teachers do many other things that we know are not dubious: they provide timely feedback, get students excited about the subject matter, go over worked examples, review previous learning, scaffold difficult tasks – and much more. All of these things that teachers do on a regular basis have plenty of empirical evidence, which shows they are effective for improving students' learning. As far as successful teaching is concerned then, it is simply important to apply a measure of common sense, to scrutinise educational practices and hold them up to the light of actual evidence. Following this line of enquiry, Part Three takes a closer look at Hattie's research into evidence-based learning, indicating key practices that successful teaching should adopt.

3. Key Points from Part One

- Teaching as a process for facilitating learning has existed since the beginning of our species. Teaching in schools, by contrast, is a relatively new phenomenon.

- Teaching is both a craft that can be taught by example and a profession, which can be understood through educational theories. It is also a vocation, a calling through which to make a positive difference to the lives of students.

- Education did not evolve as a disciplined and institutional field of study until the 19th century. Moreover, unlike other fields, education never began with commonly agreed upon canons of knowledge about subject matter or effective practice to guide teachers.

- John Dewey's impact on education has been huge in terms of influencing educators to develop a learner-centred pedagogy and a more holistic approach to education.

- Various educational initiatives and theories have gained momentum under the fundamentally false premise that they will improve learning outcomes. At best, such dubious assumptions create an unnecessary distraction for students, and at worst, they can lead to significant amounts of teaching time being lost to practices that are simply ineffective.

- In particular, there has been a strong focus in recent years on developing very broad "analytical", "critical thinking" and "problem-solving skills" – while minimising the importance placed on 'knowledge' and 'facts'. This approach, however, puts the cart before the horse; skills can only be developed in line with knowledge accumulation.

- It makes no sense to explicitly attempt to teach "21st century skills". Cognitive science has shown that all students will develop their skills naturally, hand in hand with knowledge and hard work.

- For the most part, evidence shows that teachers already do an excellent job of creating challenging lessons, providing timely feedback, getting students excited about the subject matter, going over worked examples, reviewing previous learning, scaffolding difficult tasks – and much more.

- We must remember to apply a measure of common sense, to scrutinise educational practices and hold them up to the light of actual evidence.

PART TWO

Managing Emotions

4. Human Connection

If the only tool you have is a hammer, you tend to see every problem as a nail.

- Abraham Maslow

Throughout history, human beings have inherently been social animals. Our social and emotional well-being are naturally nurtured through making and maintaining human connections. Unsurprisingly therefore, students' learning automatically benefits when they feel a human connection with the key people around them – family, peers and of course, teachers. As I often find myself saying to parents, if students are unhappy, their learning is stifled.

One need not look far for research into the importance of human connection for successful teaching and learning. Work from the child psychologist, Led Vygotsky, in the 1920s and 1930s for example, was firmly rooted in social constructivism, which stresses the significance of both culture and social environments in how we relate to the world around us (MacBlain, 2014). In other words, learning takes place through relationships with others, supported by conversation and language.

Importantly, this means that if a student does not admire or respect the teacher, s/he is far less likely to lean into difficult tasks, be enamoured with the subject or respond well to critical feedback – all natural outcomes from successful teaching. The rousing TED Talk by educator Rita Pierson (2013), for instance, makes clear this value of human connection for students. As Rita Pierson eloquently puts it, "Kids don't learn from people they don't like".

Based on research related to children's temperament and their relationships with adults, Shonkoff and Phillips (2000, pp. 237) stress the importance of secure emotional relationships with caring adults in emotional regulation and development. Moreover, Hardiman (2012, pp. 46) points to clear evidence that shows students benefit from an improvement in learning and memory when they feel supported and cared for by adults. In the subsequent sections, we look at ways in which teachers can foster a nurturing environment where all students feel connected and cared for.

Successful teaching requires the ability to connect with *and* facilitate connections between other human beings. It is also necessary for teachers and school leaders to build and foster congenial relationships across the school community, with colleagues and parents. In this way, ideas are shared, support networks are formed and a spirit of camaraderie becomes the norm.

In this section of the book, I explore the key factors that make human connection possible across the school community including values, behaviour management, extra-curricular activities, meaningful feedback, growth mindset and leadership. As with other parts of this book, these chapters can be read separately as areas of interest, or assimilated together, as part of the broader theme of 'Human Connection'. Let's look at each one of these factors in turn as they pertain to human connection.

5. Values

A key part of the work that we do as educators, is to teach children positive values such as honesty, kindness and respect. As principles that guide our thinking and behaviour, values are fundamentally important. In fact, it is not possible to have a meaningful discussion about human connection without first exploring the topic of human values. After all, values show up in how we behave and treat others.

Ideally, the teacher's relationship with students should be attuned to building not just the learner's academic profile, but also their emotional and social education too. This means that values must be well embedded in what is being taught, both implicitly (through the teacher's attitude and behaviour and explicitly (by making links through content delivery). Neil Hawkes explains it this way:

I have noted that for children to access mathematics, they need a mathematical language, to access science they need a scientific language and so on. Therefore, I think that to access ethics (a code of morality – the inner impulses, judgements and duties of people) children need to be introduced to an ethical vocabulary. Values words such as honesty, respect and trust create an ethical vocabulary, which can then act as a guide to how to live their lives. Indeed, I believe that it gives children an ethical intelligence; that is, the ability to be self-aware in order to consider their thoughts and actions, and the actions of others (Hawkes, 2013, pp. 61).

Broadly speaking there are two types of values – positive values and limiting values. Positive values include friendship, humour and reliability. Limiting values include blame, jealousy and resentment. These negative values are still values according to Barrett (2018, pp. 6), because if they were not valuable to some aspect of our psyche, we would not let them drive our behaviours. Incidentally it must also be mentioned, that although the nature of values may be universal, people differ significantly in the relative importance they attribute to values. In other words, individuals and groups have different value "priorities" (Schwartz, 2012, pp. 3).

As educators, we have a responsibility to do our best to cultivate and nurture only positive values in our students. At its most basic, this is achievable by walking the talk and practising the values that we want to see from our students. A framework of positive values should serve as an ethical and moral compass, helping to guide our interactions and reinforce our human connection with all members of the school community.

To do this authentically, we should each draw on our own unique sets of positive values. For example, one teacher might place a high value priority on creativity, fun and humour. Teaching successfully for that teacher then naturally involves channeling these values, perhaps by creating exciting learning materials and injecting humour into lessons. Two of my core values, for instance (and actually key drivers for this book), are curiosity and determination. As a teacher, I would regularly draw on my curiosity and determination, to find relatively unknown and interesting facts, which then helped to make lessons more interesting whilst serving to foster these particular values on the part of my students. It is the diversity of different values within schools that can make them such rich environments for learning.

Obviously, this requires a certain amount of self-knowledge about one's own values. If you have not already done so, it is worth exploring and asking yourself the question: What are my values? In my experience, few people take the time to really reflect on and articulate their values. Such time is well spent for anyone, especially educators, because by having a firm grip of one's own personal values, you exude significantly more authenticity – which is key for genuine human connection. There are many useful online resources which help to narrow down your top value priorities if you are unsure. I would also recommend discussing the topic of values with friends and colleagues, as it serves as good fodder for meaningful conversation and reflection about how closely you are living the values that you consider most important.

While a diversity of different value priorities among educators is healthy, there are certain positive values which all educators must possess. Students can serve as reliable barometers about what should be the most important values of teachers. In my research, as well as my conversations with students, it is clear that young people look for teachers to possess the following ten values (or some variation of these values):

- Approachability
- Commitment
- Creativity
- Fairness
- Humour
- Justice
- Kindness
- Patience
- Respect
- Sincerity

It is important to note that students will be acutely sensitive to these values – and holding steadfast to such values will go a long way in helping to establish a powerful connection with them. In the next subsection, we look at the related idea of behaviour management and strategies to cultivate this effectively in the classroom, which is also dependent on a human connection with students.

6. Effective Behaviour Management

One of the most impactful teaching strategies identified by John Hattie lies in teachers' ability to forge strong relationships with their students. This is because good teacher-student relationships are the fundamental basis for successful behaviour management. In fact, anything you can do to build a good teacher-student relationship will work in your favour when it comes to behaviour management. This can include showing a genuine interest in your students' personal hobbies, getting involved in extra-curricular activities or simply keeping up-to-date with the latest trends.

I provide in this chapter common-sense strategies that have worked successfully for me and countless numbers of other teachers who I have met. Many of the strategies I use have been inspired not just from my own experience, but also from the work of various experts on the subject. The ideas, particularly those provided by the educational writer, Sue Cowley, serve to both help foster a strong relationship with students and manage poor behaviour from students when it takes place.

To talk about successful teaching and not consider behaviour management would be short-sighted. Yet it is surprising just how little attention is given to behaviour management on teacher training courses. Effective behaviour management is the single most important foundation for successful teaching, and it is perhaps the most overlooked. Managing behaviour well is key to creating an environment in which teaching and learning can flourish, as well as helping students to understand about socially acceptable and appropriate choices. Without effective behaviour management, teaching becomes a much more stressful job. Statistics on teacher retention, for example, as we have seen at the beginning of this book, make for sober reading. Almost half of new teachers entering the profession leave within their first five years, and poor behaviour from students is, according to Education Support (Kell, 2018, pp. 12), one of the more common reasons.

Successful teachers teach not just the curriculum but also social and emotional skills. This of course, goes hand in hand with effective behaviour management. Managing behaviour well is a key ingredient for cultivating a sense of competency on the part of teachers, leading to confidence for the teacher in his or her abilities and a more satisfying career.

Managing behaviour well requires three overlapping qualities: emotional competence, an understanding of human thinking and excellent organisation.

Emotional competence

Managing behaviour is an emotional skill; it requires training yourself to think and act in a certain way, which for most of us goes against the grain of how we would instinctively respond to poor behaviour from students. This means that when a child misbehaves, you do not lose your temper and you show emotion only sparingly. Likewise, you do not use prizes such as sweets or toys in an attempt to manipulate children to meet your minimum expectations, i.e. simply for behaving well. In my early days of teaching, I occasionally did lose my temper and I did give out unnecessary prizes – and in both scenarios, I failed miserably. While such approaches may work in the short-term, the long-term costs are too high.

As a classroom teacher, you must learn to take ownership of and master your emotions – a point to which I will return again and again in this book. The importance of this idea has been known for thousands of years. It was in the 1st century that the stoic philosopher, Epictetus said: "No man is free who does not master himself." Similarly, in the 15th century, Leonardo da Vinci put it this way: "One can have no smaller or greater mastery than mastery of oneself." Their rationale, I believe, is that in a lowered emotional state, you will only be able to see problems rather than solutions. When you are in a higher emotional state, you will communicate high expectations of students in terms of both their achievement and behaviour. Your emotions and nonverbal cues have significant implications for your classroom's success. (For specific ideas and tools to help you develop your emotional competence, you may skip ahead to chapter 10, which explores mindfulness.)

To cite one example, a 1993 study by Nalini Ambady and Robert Rosenthal found that humans do indeed communicate a significant information about themselves through nonverbal signals such as body language and facial expressions. Moreover, others can form quick, accurate impressions of a person based on these nonverbal signals. Specifically, their research used video clips between 6 seconds to 30 seconds in length to show 'thin slices of nonverbal behavior' of different teachers. When students were shown the clips, they could quickly and accurately determine the effectiveness of the different teachers filmed – without any prior knowledge of the teacher.

Essentially, the snap judgements those students made aligned with judgements made by students who had spent several months observing the same teachers. For anyone who makes a profession involving public speaking – which is all educators – these findings are remarkable. They show, in no uncertain terms, just how quickly and accurately students size up a teacher upon their first encounter in the classroom.

The point is your facial expressions and body language are extremely important in determining how your students see you and your ability to manage their behaviour. If you do not feel confident, fake it until you make it. Move around the classroom naturally and purposefully (like you own it), stand tall and exert a conscious effort to make eye contact with each and every learner. You should work to cultivate a strong sense of inner calm, remaining unfazed even when things go wrong. Accordingly, your tone of voice should be calm, neutral and assertive, which communicates that you are in control and you will get what you expect.

In addition to your nonverbal cues, it is important to consider your choice of words. In this regard, there are four key characteristics of an emotionally

34

competent teacher:

1. **An emphasis on positive statements rather than negative statements**, e.g. "We've got some exciting activities to do today." Do your best to frame everything you say in a positive light even when students make mistakes. Highlighting students' successes (rather than focusing on mistakes) helps to build both their self-esteem and your relationship with them. In particular, by looking for and focusing on those children who are behaving well, you are likely to make that behaviour the norm in your classroom.

2. **Regular and sustained use of praise**, e.g. "As per usual, you're working incredibly quietly Class 5. Well done!"

3. **Teaching students the social skills they need to be successful.** Use 'I expect...' statements, to set children positive behaviour targets, e.g. "I expect you to show respect for everyone in our class, paying full attention when someone else is speaking." Communicating clear expectations and sharing these regularly with your class is a key part of successful behaviour management. This is particularly important in your first few lessons with a new class, when you will need to define the boundaries between what is acceptable and unacceptable behaviour.

4. **Build a rapport with the parents.** Outside of school, parents or caregivers will have the biggest influence on the behaviour of the children in your class. It is helpful therefore to build a respectful relationship with them so that when behaviour issues do arise you will have their full support. Occasionally, you may also need to stand your ground with pushy parents who side with the version of events given by their child.

When you display the above characteristics in your practice, you are more likely to have your students' full engagement. This is because emotional competence and ensuring full engagement on the part of your students go hand in hand; it is impossible to have one without the other.

In order to cultivate emotional competence, it is necessary to regulate your internal dialogue and emotions. The words from the influential book 'The Power of Positive Thinking' by Norman Vincent Peale are relevant:

Feelings of confidence depend on the type of thoughts that habitually occupy your mind. Think defeat and you are bound to be defeated... Formulate and stamp indelibly on your mind a mental picture of yourself as succeeding. (Peale, 1953, pp. 16-17)

By regulating your emotions in such a way, you will be able to project what Derington & Goddard refer to as 'resolute optimism', which is contagious and has an energising impact on those around you:

The teacher who enters a classroom in a warm, appreciative and enthusiastic manner with obvious high expectation is likely to have this reflected back by the students.
(Derrington & Goddard, 2008, pp. 27)

Just like a muscle, maintaining resolute optimism requires constant training to begin each day with a positive frame of mind. The power of one's internal monologue cannot be overstated. All personal development is based on moving our inner voice away from self-criticism and negativity to a more positive and affirming self-talk. As Beck et al. (2003) point out, this approach is grounded in a well-known cognitive therapy technique and psychotherapeutic practice in which individuals learn how to distinguish between realistic and maladaptive thinking.

One of the fundamental messages from Dave Burgess's book, *Teach Like a Pirate*, is the importance of exuding passion as a way to fuel student engagement. An interesting and insightful point that Dave Burgess makes is that this passion need not necessarily come from a love of the subject matter itself – instead it can come from professional or personal passion alone:

For example, I mentioned that I am not passionate about railroads. Fortunately for my students, I am passionate about developing engaging presentations for my material. So, although I might not be jazzed about the subject, I can absolutely be inspired and fully engaged in my attempt to present the topic in an entertaining way. (Burgess, 2012, pp. 12)

Another way to incorporate more passion into your practice is to remind yourself of why you wanted to work in education. You decided to make a positive difference to the lives of your students. Whether you realise it or not, they can make a positive difference in your life too. Do not bemoan about having a difficult class. Skills do come from struggle. When I reflect on the children that I have taught over the years, it has been the most challenging of these children that have helped me grow the most. By reminding yourself then of both the value you can bring and the personal growth you can achieve in teaching, you will more likely feel that you are living with purpose – and nothing will enhance your performance more than the feeling of living with purpose. Consequently, finding ways to incorporate your passions into your teaching practice will energise you, ensuring that you can create powerful and engaging lessons which are more likely to be remembered.

Of course, when it comes to energy levels you need to look after yourself. This means taking exercising after work to relieve stress, getting plenty of rest and making sure that you stay well hydrated. Sleep, in particular, can be one of the most productive things you can do when considering its rejuvenation benefits. I would also recommend careful time management. It can be easy to fall into a trap of saying 'yes' to every demand on your time, particularly at the beginning of your career, e.g. student council, extra-curricular activities, fundraising projects, etc. However, it is important that you learn to politely say 'no' in order to avoid too many demands being placed on you. By doing so, you will have the energy to focus on what is most important – your teaching.

Regulating learners' emotional well-being

Once you have mastered your emotional competence, you are in a position to regulate the emotional competence of your students. It should be obvious that one of the most important influences on your students' behaviour is what you say to them. This is because what you say to students, especially about their performance, greatly affects their self-talk and ultimately their behaviour .

One of the most controversial research studies in this area was carried out in 1939 at the University of Iowa. Psychology professor, Wendell Johnson, and graduate student, Mary Tudor, conducted an experiment with 22 orphans, to determine whether a child with a stutter could be convinced to abandon it and, conversely, whether a non-stuttering speaker could be induced to stutter. They separated the children into four groups: (1) stutterers who were told their speech was fine, (2) stutterers who were told they had a speech problem, (3) non-stuttering speakers who were told they had serious problems with their speech, and (4) non-stuttering speakers who were told their speech was fine. By the end of the experiment, all the groups' speech was unchanged *except* for group (3), the non-stuttering children who were told they had serious speech problems. For these children, including formerly outgoing and sociable individuals, they became anxious, withdrawn and unwilling to speak for fear of making a mistake. Tudor made the following observations of the six children in this group:

All of the subjects . . . showed similar types of speech behavior during the experimental period. A decrease in verbal output of all six subjects; that is they were reluctant to speak and spoke only when they were urged to. Second, their rate of speaking was decreased. They spoke more slowly and with greater exactness. They had a tendency to weigh each word before they said it. Third, the length of response was shorter. The two younger subjects responded with one word whenever possible. Fourth, they were more self-conscious. They appeared shy and embarrassed in many situations. Fifth, they accepted the fact that there was something definitely wrong with their speech. Sixth, every subject reacted to his speech interruptions in some manner. Some hung their heads: others gasped and covered their mouths with their hands; others laughed with embarrassment. In every case the children's behavior changed noticeably. (Tudor, 1939, pp. 147- 148)

Dubbed the "Monster Study" by Johnson's peers who were horrified he would conduct such an experiment, this study remained unknown and unpublished for several decades. It seems likely that Johnson himself was embarrassed about the long-term harm it caused the participants from the aforementioned group (Silverman, 1988).

While the findings of the study provide strong evidence that diagnosing normal disfluency as stuttering can cause stuttering, it also serves to show the powerful impact that teachers have on their students' self-confidence and self-image. Again, I cannot emphasise enough how important it is to be positive, not only with your internal dialogue but also with the dialogue you have with students. Unfortunately, I have too often seen teachers engage in a teaching style or disciplinary practice that induces stress in students and consequently inhibits their learning. Sadly, it is not uncommon for some teachers to give negative or embarrassing feedback to a student in front of his or her peers, even inadvertently. Invariably, such situations in the classroom can impact the student's self-esteem, behaviour and willingness to participate in learning activities.

Pekrun, Goetz, Titz, and Perry (2002) conducted a series of studies to determine the emotions that students say they experience during the school day. Significantly, the most frequent emotion identified was anxiety, accounting for up to 25% of all emotions reported. Behavioural problems associated with anxiety have also been observed (Ruttle et al., 2011). The research shows that when anxiety-driven behavioural problems begin, cortisol levels become abnormally elevated, which ultimately leads to poor academic performance.

There is clearly an interplay between behaviour, cognition and emotion. Teachers should understand the influence of emotions, both positive and negative, on attention, memory and higher-order thinking. Research demonstrates the negative effects of stress on learning from prenatal stages to childhood, adolescent and adult learning. Positive emotions, conversely, have been shown to improve learning outcomes (Hardiman, 2012, pp. 27). Teachers must therefore set the emotional climate of the classroom to promote a joyful and safe learning environment. Activities must be planned purposefully such that they provide students with an emotional connection

38

to the content, making the subject matter more personal, relevant and meaningful.

Getting the right background sounds

In order to facilitate learners' emotional well-being and help create an environment conducive to learning, it helps if the teacher takes control of background noise as much as possible. As one might expect, classrooms with poor behaviour tend to be noisier classrooms. Smyth (1979) studied the effects of noise on children's ability to recall information. His research showed that children in noisy classrooms had significantly worse performance than those in quiet classrooms, with the greatest disparity occurring with younger children.

In contrast to the effects of typical classroom background noise, music has been shown time and again to have soothing effects (Giles, 1990). Although classical music is often used in this way, other musical genres can be equally effective. I would regularly use pop music as a tool to help foster positive emotions whilst students were working. Particularly at the beginning of the school year, I found that tracks such as 'Here Comes the Sun' by the Beatles or 'Downtown' by Petula Clark, gave the classroom a welcoming and positive atmosphere. Nowadays it is very easy with applications like Spotify, Shazam and YouTube, to put together your unique classroom playlist.

Understanding how humans think

Developing behaviour management skills requires a basic understanding of how humans think – the things humans do to avoid what they dislike, and to get things they like. This understanding should be used by teachers to create a system of praise and sanctions, which motivates children to behave well because it feels good to do so. There are many options here including point systems, marbles in a jar, extra playtime and so on. One of my favourite strategies is to phone home to share some positive comments about the child. This works particularly well for those students who are keen to please their parents.

It is worth remembering too that children will follow the model you set for them. If you say thank you all the time then even without realising it children will emulate your politeness. In particular, "thank you" works well when coupled with a short direction delivered in a calm tone, e.g. "Lydia, please be quiet. Turn around and finish your work, thank you." Giving a direct instruction like this, and following it with "thank you", implies that you expect the student to follow your instruction. I have found that establishing a climate of good manners helps tremendously to build a cohesive and positive classroom.

On the other hand, if you shout to get children's attention, they will learn to shout too. This in turn leads to a noisier working environment, which will only serve to heighten your stress levels and theirs. As far as possible then, in times when you need to get children's attention, use non-verbal signals, for instance:

- Raising your hand in the air;
- Ringing a bell;
- Clapping three times.

Once children become accustomed with your non-verbal signal(s), they should become hard-wired into their subconscious. It should feel as though you are using a magic wand every time you use your chosen non-verbal signal, as a sense of calm and quiet should quickly descend across the classroom.

However tempting it may be, raising your voice really is unnecessary. If you have a clear system of consequences, there is no need to shout; just calmly state what will happen if the poor behaviour continues and let the consequence do its work. If you absolutely must shout, which I actually often enjoy doing, make sure it is for something positive. Shouting to celebrate that Ian was completely silent during the whole assembly (and I like to do this with a stern look on my face) gets everyone's attention, makes Ian feel great about himself and helps you feel positive as well. It might sound strange (and to onlookers, it certainly is strange), but it works every time at replicating more of the positive behaviour that you want to see.

In terms of content delivery, as obvious as it may sound, unless the subject matter is delivered in an interesting way, children will quickly lose concentration. As a rough guide, Sue Cowley (2012, pp. 24) suggests that children can concentrate for their age in minutes plus two. Thus, a five-year-old will only be able to concentrate for approximately seven minutes on one activity. With such a short timeframe, it is necessary that you do your best to hold the children's attention.

Among the many options at your disposal to hold students' attention, your best tool is your voice. You should aim to vary the tone and pitch of your voice, putting emphasis on key words. By doing so, you will hold students' attention for much longer. By contrast, a monotone will quickly lead to boredom and misbehaviour. The teacher, Christopher Emdin makes an excellent demonstration of this point, in his TED Talk, 'Teach teachers how to create magic'. In my experience, I have found that sudden, unexpected pauses in the middle of a sentence helps to keep a certain suspense, which serves to make your delivery more gripping.

Concision is essential. This applies both to your teaching delivery and any general instructions you give. It is worth mentioning that this can be one of the biggest challenges for some teachers, especially those who love the sound of their own voices. However, the less you say, the easier it is for your students to assimilate, remember and act on what you have said. Conversely, the longer you talk, the more likely you will lose students to boredom and misbehaviour.

For particularly tough classes, it pays to get the support from the "ringleaders". From experience, I would say that your best allies for behaviour management are actually the students who would otherwise be the most rebellious, defiant and demanding – as long as you can get them on your side. As Plevin explains:

Relationships with these students can take time to build but tough ringleaders tend to have an in-built psychological need for attention and recognition. By asking them directly

41

for their assistance, you give them the acknowledgement and appreciation they crave, while quickly developing a level of mutual trust and respect. (2016, pp. 25)

I have used this strategy on several occasions. On one occasion, an entire year group was lining up improperly at the end of breaktimes. After the usual strategies proved ineffective (reprimands and reducing their breaktime the following period), I decided to try something new. I enlisted the help of the two most unruly children from each class to be a line monitor. Every single one of them – after having it explained in private why they were the ideal candidates – jumped at the opportunity to prove how effective they could be in the role. I made it clear to them, lining up was becoming a serious problem, and we needed the very best students to demonstrate maturity, popularity and high standards – key qualities of any effective line monitor! The problems with lining up vanished the following day.

I used the same strategy when we had a problem across several year groups with swearing and bad language in the playground. I set the scene by talking with the children during an assembly about how disappointed and saddened I felt that such language would be used. I then called several of the children (who were the most notorious for using bad language) into my office. Having discussed with these "ringleaders" the problem and their ideas for what we could do, I made my request. I told each of them that they would make an excellent swearword monitor. These students relished the acknowledgement and appreciation they were receiving and were quick to accept their positions. As these children held a certain authority and influence by virtue of their popularity, they had an incredibly positive impact in curtailing swearing and bad language in school.

Of course, the key to making this particular strategy work, as with many similar approaches, is to make sure that you have first built a relationship based on mutual respect beforehand. Disappointingly, there are teachers who will humiliate or embarrass children as a punishment for when they misbehave. While this approach might work in the short term (for all the wrong reasons), it is an unfair way of dealing with the problem and will only serve to foster resentment in the long term.

Organisation

The classroom should be a home away from home with predictable routines and structured activities. It is within this environment that children should know the boundaries for acceptable and unacceptable behaviour. For students, this provides a much-needed sense of consistency and stability.

This requires first and foremost that you explain to your students the basics, for example, of how you expect them to enter the room, line up, leave the classroom, present work in books and so on. It may well be necessary to walk through every single detail of classroom procedure several times, especially for younger students. If you are new to teaching, notes or an outline before the beginning of each school day will help you internalise the classroom procedures and expectations for yourself. By having your procedures and expectations clear in your own mind, you will be much quicker to identify and respond appropriately to any poor behaviour.

Consistency

Most schools have expectations and rules for uniform. In the same way that you should strictly monitor the presentation of your students' work in their books, you must be a stickler for ensuring that students' appearance conforms with school expectations. I can remember from my early days of teaching being somewhat bemused by more experienced teachers who would show genuine disappointment of any student who made so much as the slightest deviation away from school expectations in terms of their work presentation (e.g. writing in a different coloured pen than the norm), or school uniform (wearing a tie slightly too short). These teachers would go to enormous lengths to correct what in their eyes was misconduct, following through with stern warnings, reprimands and all manner of sanctions. At the time, I honestly thought that such reactions to small details like this were over the top and did not have anything to do with student learning. As I gained more experience in teaching though, I came to understand that small details do matter. It is reinforcing what students value most: fairness and equity. As well as helping students to feel part of their community, paying attention to the small details of what is acceptable and unacceptable, goes a long way to foster students' respect for authority, rules and expectations.

When you do have to reprimand or issue sanctions for poor behaviour choices, it must be consistent. (Ideally, behaviour expectations and consequences for misbehaviour will be consistent across the school). All students need to know that if they are not doing what they should be, there will be consequences – and that everyone will be treated the same way. If, for example, you let Vicky doodle with a pen all over her hand, you send an unconscious signal to Vicky (and her friends) that this is acceptable. If other students witness her behaviour going unchallenged, they will feel they can do the same.

Seating plans are an effective way to help you further demonstrate organisation and keep control. As well as helping you to learn names at the beginning of the academic year, it sends a signal that you are organised, orderly and in charge. As shown in the photos below, sticky notes are ideal for marking out seating arrangements. For younger children (8 years and below), I would use them on the carpet (for the introductory part of a lesson, plenary or story time) and on the floor outside the classroom to indicate where children should sit when lining up. The sticky notes do wear away after a few weeks, but students will remember the seating plan well before then.

I believe strongly that order and beauty are key components of a classroom that fosters a high standard of behaviour. In my experience, cluttered, untidy and messy classrooms engender poorer levels of student behaviour. Tidying your desk at the end of each day can go a long way, to help keeping you in a "tidy mindset" for other parts of the classroom. This in turn will benefit students' behaviour and concentration.

An online behaviour management system such as Class Dojo can help you to further manage your classroom by providing a point system which awards points for positive student behaviours. It is also a great way to get parents involved, helping to ensure that they are not only aware of their child's behaviour but also have an idea of the good work their child is producing.

It should go without saying that lessons need to be planned thoroughly. All students should be appropriately challenged with meaningful lesson activities and have extra tasks to move onto if they finish work early. Before lessons begin, it helps to have a calming activity for students when they first enter your room such as word problems or maths puzzles. This ensures there is as little downtime as possible.

Managing misbehaviour

When positive influence and organisation fail to maintain student behaviour – which inevitably will happen – it is necessary to manage the negative choices that students make. This should be done by following clearly defined, hierarchical consequences. Although there is not a neat step-by-step method that fits all situations or all children, you should have in mind (and on display) a clear sequence of consequences to carry out in the event of misbehaviour.

Assuming low-level behaviour issues (e.g. shouting out when the teacher is talking), below is a suggested sequence:

1. The first time a student calls out, give a warning and/or take away a class point.

2. The second time the student calls out, s/he will move seats.

3. The third time the student calls out, deduct 10-minutes of breaktime.

4. The fourth time the student calls out, deduct all of breaktime.

5. If the behaviour issues continue after this point, then a meeting with the parents/caregivers should be arranged.

There are a whole range of sanctions that can be applied, such as loss of privileges, detentions (reflection time), phone calls/emails to parents and so on. The important point is that your sanctions should start at a low level and gradually increase if the student continues to defy you. You should also remember the importance of consistency here. If your rule on not finishing work is that students have to stay behind at breaktime to finish it, then this sanction must be applied. If you do not follow up, then you may as well not bother with having the rule in the first place. Yes, this can be time-consuming in the short term, but always staying consistent by following through with your stated consequences will pay off in the long term.

Common sense is obviously required here and this sequence will need to be adapted for the situation at hand. In the event of a student who physically harms another student or swears in class, you would undoubtedly escalate directly to steps 4 and 5. Remember, whatever the situation, do your best to remain relentlessly calm and polite, which makes confrontations with students less likely to occur.

When students do cause problems in your lessons, it is also imperative that you keep excellent records. For every lesson, you should record exactly what a student has said and/or done to disrupt the class. You then have a document which can be used for evidence should you need to show parents or colleagues.

Keep parents in the loop

As mentioned in the section about emotional competence, there will be times when you need to escalate by making contact with the parents or caregivers. The role of parents in terms of influencing their child's behaviour should not be underestimated. Most of the time you will have their support when behaviour issues arise, especially if you have already built a strong rapport with them. I include discussion on this topic in the organisation section here, because, just like a detective, you will need to be organised and gather all facts (and, when necessary, apologies) prior to contacting the parents.

Here is an example of a typical email that I would send to parents following a behaviour incident in the playground:

Dear Parents,

Please be aware that your son, Brian was involved in a fight earlier today during the lunchtime break with another boy from his class, Peter. I understand this fight began because of a misunderstanding over table football, as Brian felt left out. Apparently, both boys had sworn at one another and were physically aggressive. Another boy, from Class 4, then intervened in an attempt to break up the fight and got hurt.

Both Brian and Peter admit they were at fault and have apologised for their poor behaviour. Fortunately, neither Brian nor Peter were badly hurt. Nevertheless, it is important to remind the boys of the seriousness of their behaviour and ensure that it is not repeated in the future.

As with all behaviour incidents at this level, this will be recorded on our school behaviour system, and the boys will miss their breaktimes tomorrow, to reflect on what has happened. Obviously, if there are any future incidents like this from either of the boys, then this will be met with more serious consequences.

In the meantime, I would be particularly grateful if you can talk with Brian about what has happened. It is especially important for Brian to be mindful of the language he uses at school, as we strive to ensure that everyone in our school community is treated with kindness and respect.

Thank you in advance for your support.

Kind regards,

Mr Will

Such behaviour incidents of physical aggression are common in schools, and they tend to be more common the younger children are. Over the last decade, I have probably dealt with the aftermath of at least several hundred fights and other acts of physical violence directed by students towards other students – usually in the playground but sometimes in the classroom.

Although parents are often shocked by such behaviour (and this can be its own challenge), it should not come as a surprise; children, especially when they are very young, are still in the process of developing their abilities to self-regulate and can resort to aggressive behaviour when angry.

In this particular case, I also needed to contact the parents of the boy from Class 4 who tried to help break up the fight. As with all "exciting" situations like these, children are very quick to tell their parents what happened (or at least their version of what happened) during the school day. Parents are generally looking to see how the school will respond to misconduct. As far as is necessary, the parents of all children involved should be kept in the loop:

Dear Parents,

I would like to make you both aware of an incident involving David, which took place earlier today.

This afternoon there was a fight between two Class 3 boys during the lunchtime break. Unfortunately, David got involved in an attempt to help break up the fight and was smacked in the face. David was then immediately taken to the school nurse and thankfully was not seriously hurt.

Please rest assured that the two boys who David tried to help, are currently facing serious consequences for their poor behaviour. However, you may wish to reinforce the message at home, for David not to get involved if he witnesses another incident like this in the future. Instead, he should just call a member of staff.

If you have any concerns or questions about this incident, please do not hesitate to contact me.

Kind regards,

Mr Will

Any such communication with parents must come across as unemotional and clearly state the facts about what happened as well as any follow-up action taken. The names of other children should only be mentioned if appropriate to do so. Sometimes your communication with parents will also require that you arrange a meeting with them to follow up on the incident. Such communication and meetings are an important part of the teacher's role.

There will be other times when you need to stand your ground with parents or caregivers. It is not uncommon for teachers to be reluctant to reprimand students for fear of unpleasant confrontations with parents. For this reason, it is vital to have the support of school leadership when dealing with behaviour issues. I particularly like this letter written to parents by the headmaster, Bruce Grindlay, of Sutton Valance School in Kent, England, which is a good example of what support for teachers should look like:

Dear Parents and Guardians

At the heart of the relationship that exists between the School and its parents is the understanding that we have the long-term interests of your sons and daughters in common. I am writing to ask for your co-operation and understanding in not immediately challenging staff who have seen fit to raise a behavioural concern or impose a sanction on your child. Last term, dealing with these took up a disproportionate amount of time and energy from staff who should be spending their non-teaching time preparing lessons and marking. It has become an issue for staff and some are preferring not to sanction a child for fear of time-consuming and unpleasant repercussions.

We must remember that we are the adults in this triangular relationship (School, parent and pupil) and that the School is a deeply caring and nurturing environment. We are all trying to do what is best for your child. We do not relish telling children off and imposing sanctions; it is not our style to make children unhappy, but it is necessary at times.

Please can I ask you to not always believe your child's version of events? It is necessary to remember that we were not present at the time and, if truth be told, who has most at stake: a child who has got something wrong or the adult teacher simply pointing out and dealing with misbehaviour or poor conduct?

Children will get things wrong and that is fine if they learn from it. You have chosen Sutton Valence as you like its ethos and what it does to educate your child; that means that the School's expectations, my expectations, need to be maintained. We all need to abide by these expectations if Sutton Valence is to achieve all it sets out to do.

I understand that consistency is the key and staff, as human beings, are not always consistent. However, I am sure that there would be greater consistency of approach if they felt that you would support their sanctions and decisions in the first instance.

Can I respectfully ask that if you have an issue with a decision and really think it needs challenging, then please do not take this up with the staff, but make an appointment via my P.A. to see me instead? The staff are merely upholding my expectations and I need them to do this and then to get on with their core priority: educating your children.

With best wishes

As parents form a key part of the school community, it helps to involve them in the education of their children – especially in situations where there has been misconduct. Where appropriate, I like to use misconducts as opportunities to involve the parents in the teaching process, by encouraging them to talk to their children about positive values. Consider this example:

Dear Parents,

Please be aware that there was an incident involving your son, Gary in which he broke into the locker of another student, Victoria from his class.

Although I accept Gary's explanation that he did not intend to steal anything from Victoria's locker, it was nonetheless an invasion of Victoria's privacy (and involved him stealing her locker password).

In school, we work hard to teach students the importance of positive values such as kindness, honesty and respect. I would be grateful therefore, if you could also discuss this incident with your son.

As a consequence for Gary's behaviour, he will not be allowed to use his locker for the next 2-weeks. In addition, Gary will be required to spend Monday lunchtime with me, to complete a reflection activity related to this incident.

I trust you will understand how important it is that these consequences are implemented, and I appreciate any reinforcement of positive values that you can provide at home.

Please do not hesitate to get in touch if you have any concerns or questions.

Kind regards,

Mr Will

When presented with the facts and being called upon to help treat the misconduct as a teaching opportunity for their child, most parents respond very well. You will notice in this particular example, that I talk about a "reflection activity" for Gary. For all intents and purposes, this is code for 'detention'. Before giving a detention, some key points must be kept in mind.

Key considerations about detention

Detentions have long been a staple disciplinary measure in schools in order to manage misbehaviour. However, detention is also quite a contentious policy, and educators find themselves divided on their feelings about its effectiveness. The main criticism held against detentions is that, while they may serve as a deterrent for behaving poorly, they do not actually change students' behaviour (McCann, 2017, pp. 6). I can testify from my own experience of holding traditional detentions in which students simply lose time, at best they only serve to show students that there is a consequence for their poor behaviour but in themselves do not achieve much more. At worst, they serve to foster resentment on both the part of the student and sometimes even the teacher towards the student because of the time lost.

This has led me to adapt detention time such that it is based on a more restorative than punitive justice system. I no longer call it detention but instead 'reflection time'. The idea is to actually use the time to have some discussion with the students about their misconduct and to ensure the students are aware of why there had to be a consequence. Grazak (2013) speaks highly of this type of detention, which apparently is most beneficial at the middle school level. By allowing students to talk about what is going on in their life, it provides a good opportunity for teachers to connect with the students. It can also be a useful time for them to discuss other issues such as grades, attendance and activities in school. As long as the detention time is used productively, it not only serves as a deterrent for poor behaviour but also can improve students' behaviour outcomes in the long run.

7. Teaching Boys

The teaching of boys and adolescents deserves special consideration, as for at least the last two decades, there has been increasing concern that boys are falling behind in formal education. Instinctive differences between boys and girls are well-documented in various educational, psychological and sociological studies. Among many distinctions, it is widely recognised that, generally speaking, boys are more challenging to discipline than girls – and boys are less interested in formal education. Simply put, boys tend to be more restless, disruptive and prone to distraction than girls.

Statistics show that the majority of school exclusions tend to be boys.[2] As well as behaviour problems being more prevalent with boys than girls, it has been demonstrated repeatedly that girls outperform boys in academics (e.g. Mieke Van Houtte, 2004). International data shows that in 70 percent of countries, girls outperform boys in every curricular subject – including countries where girls' access to education is severely restricted.[3] Perhaps unsurprisingly, female university students and graduates worldwide now far outnumber their male counterparts – a trend that shows no sign of changing.[4]

---

[2] Statistics from the UK Department for Education show that boys tend to be excluded three times more, on average, than girls:
https://www.gov.uk/government/collections/statistics-exclusions

[3] https://www.sciencedaily.com/releases/2015/01/150126125015.htm

[4] Across OECD (Organisation for Economic Cooperation & Development) countries show greater female to male ratios in higher education:
http://www.oecd.org/about/membersandpartners/

For the most part, the facts and statistics about the underperformance of boys are well-known. What is not so widely acknowledged though, is how modern life can be more problematic for boys than girls – particularly within the formal education system. The problem, according to Sue Palmer (2009) in her book, *21st Century Boys*, is that we currently live in an 'electronic village' – a marketing and screen-based culture which inhibits healthy eating, good sleep routines and free play – from an early age. While these trends affect all children, they tend to more negatively impact boys. Many youngsters, especially boys, seem to be pursuing what Sue Palmer calls a 'loss of the mind' – the erosion of conscious identity through technological fixes and distractions.

The issues for boys are very real. This is important for teachers to realise in order to have greater levels of empathy and understanding for the males in their classrooms. Boys have a greater likelihood of suffering not just from academic and behavioural problems, but also intrinsic learning challenges. For instance, the ratio of boys to girls experiencing the following developmental disorders shows a marked disparity:

- ADHD & dyspraxia   4:1

- Reading problems   3:1

- Asperger syndrome   9:1

Evolutionary biology might help to explain some of the differences we see in the classroom in terms of behaviour. Over time, males have proven to be significantly more competitive, violent, and risk-loving than females.. In the classroom of course, these tendencies manifest as more rambunctious and restless behaviours on the part of the boys. In terms of emotional problems, Sami Tamimi (2005) notes:

'The big difference is that boys externalise their problems and it comes out as bad behaviour – girls tend to internalise it, as sadness. Boys' issues are therefore issues for others, not just themselves.'

This externalisation of poor behaviour matters not just in the classroom but for society at large. As Sue Palmer (2009, pp. 4) states 'if boys aren't reasonably civilised, confident and able to exercise self-control by the time they reach their teens, they can become a problem for society: four out of five criminal offences are committed by males.' Policymakers in the United States for example, have calculated that if just 5 percent more boys completed secondary school and matriculated to college, the U.S. would save $8 billion a year in welfare and criminal justice costs (Reichert &

52

Hawley, 2010, xi).

There are several strategies teachers can initiate to at least mitigate the particular issues facing boys. First and foremost, it is important that teachers coach parents on appropriate measures to take at home. At a minimum, parents ought to provide the following:

- Nutritious food

- A safe home

- Plenty of sleep and exercise

- Attention and love

- Discipline that teaches (and is not permissive or punitive)

This might sound like common sense, but it cannot be assumed that all parents are doing these things. Most parents, in my experience, do not put limits on their children's screen time. Many children have a computer and/or television in the bedroom – with no restrictions on their use. It is also normal for a great many children to gorge on fast food and sugary beverages. Teachers must therefore use workshops and parent-teacher conferences to advise parents to limit their children's use of screens and to make sure healthy food is regularly provided for them.

For lesson delivery, there are at least four approaches which I have found particularly appropriate for boys:

Physical movement - During my several years of teaching first graders (6 to 7-year olds), I would periodically get them jumping up and down for two minutes at least twice a day. I would play music during this time and make it a competition to see who could jump the highest! The idea of course, was simply to get the class (specifically, the boys) to expend as much energy as possible. Immediately afterward, the children would approach their classroom activities much calmer.

Competition - Boys naturally tend to be more competitive than girls – and nothing gets them more excited and engaged than a good competition. Quizzes, games and projects can all be easily embedded into the teaching process. Online resources such as Quizlet and Kahoot are good choices to use at the beginning of the lesson or as part of the plenary.

Hands-on learning refers to learning by doing. Activities that get students making or constructing can help them think critically about what they are learning while teaching them the design process and problem solving. STEAM activities and Makerspaces offer good places to start with hands-on learning. See Chapters 32 and 33 for more information.

Flexibility - As with all learners, irrespective of gender, it is important to remain flexible. But it tends to be boys in particular who do not appear to be natural learners in the formal educational setting. Boys may show little interest in completing worksheets, working cooperatively with others or reading the class text. Differentiation, however, can circumvent their more difficult responses. Having taught boys with Attention Deficit Hyperactivity Disorder (ADHD) and Oppositional Defiant Disorder (ODD) for example, I know first-hand what frustrating challenges these issues can present for the teacher. In such situations, I have found it necessary to establish special learning stations, in which certain students can work freely on tasks and challenges that interest them. Although these students may not always work on the same learning objectives as others in the classroom, this is precisely what it means to be flexible and differentiate.

8. Child Protection & Safeguarding

I often think of the role of an educator as akin to a "practical psychologist". Nowhere is this more important than in the area of child protection and safeguarding. These terms deserve some discussion because they can be related to students' behaviour, and they are fundamental aspects of any teacher's role.

First, let's clarify the terms:

- *Safeguarding* refers to the measures taken to protect and promote the well-being and safety of all members of the school community.

- *Child protection* refers to the processes undertaken to protect children who have been identified as suffering, or being at risk of suffering, significant harm or neglect.

Occasionally, child protection and safeguarding issues will crop up and sometimes this can manifest as poor behaviour, which ultimately requires a completely different attitude and approach. As child protection is thankfully an area that has garnered more attention in recent years, it is generally well covered on teacher training courses and many schools globally now have strict guidance and procedures to follow when it comes to these matters.

For teachers (and all staff working on behalf of young people), child protection and safeguarding simply require that they both respect and protect young people in the school. Although not pleasant topics to address, educators must have some awareness of the key categories of abuse:

Physical abuse

This involves causing physical harm to a young person. Physical harm may also be caused when a parent or caregiver fabricates the symptoms or deliberately induces an illness in the young person.

Emotional abuse

This is the persistent emotional maltreatment of a young person. Emotional abuse can make the young person feel rejected, worthless or inadequate.

Sexual abuse

This may involve physical contact or non-contact activities, for example, encouraging a young person to look at sexual images.

Radicalisation

There are many definitions and types of radicalisation. However, in the school context, radicalisation refers to leading individuals towards a terrorist ideology. In the case of Islamic terrorism for example, indicators may include a change in ideas, such as the sudden adoption of religious clothing, growing a beard, introversion, cutting links with friends or even visiting a conflict zone.

Neglect

This is by far the most common category of abuse by parents or caregivers. It generally involves the persistent failure to meet the young persons' basic physical or psychological needs.

Much more common than abuse by adults towards young people, is peer-on-peer abuse. Again, this can take many forms, including:

- **physical abuse**;

- **sexually harmful behaviour** such as inappropriate sexual language or touching;

- **sexting,** including pressuring another person to send sexual imagery;

- **prejudiced behaviour** - a range of behaviours that causes someone to feel powerless or excluded and which relates to themes such as belonging and identity.

We must remember that young people sometimes behave the way they do because of issues they are facing either in their social lives at school or with their families outside of school. When it comes to a student's individual circumstances, it is necessary to exercise common sense and astute judgement when something seems amiss. The child touching another child inappropriately, the sight of unusual bruises or self-harm scars, the child smelling of urine, the sudden weight loss or erratic behaviour – all of these sorts of things must be reported and followed up, ensuring the child's dignity and privacy is respected.

Individual indicators though, will rarely, on their own, provide conclusive evidence. Indeed, many of these indicators are typical of child/adolescent behaviour in some stage of their development. The indicators have to be viewed together, with each small piece of information helping to inform how best to act.

In the event that a student suffering from abuse approaches you to make a disclosure, there are several important steps to be followed. As the person responsible in this situation, you should:

• Find a safe location;

• Ensure there is visual access and an open door in one-to-one situations;

• Listen carefully and seriously at the student's pace;

• Use open language such as "tell me", or "describe to me";

• Make a careful record of what was said ensuring the following have been answered: Who was involved? What happened? When did it happen? Where did it happen?

The adult should never:

• Ask leading question or offer opinions;

• Examine an injury or take photos;

• Make promises to the student about confidentiality;

On the rare occasions when I have had to deal with child protection concerns, I have worked with a skilled and trustworthy leadership team who have helped me to navigate these issues. Any decent school will provide child protection training and should know what to look out for and how to proactively help with handling such issues if they arise. In difficult circumstances, the value of an effective working relationship with your colleagues and parents can make all the difference. The next subsection explores the topic of managing your relationships with colleagues and parents in more detail.

9. Managing Colleagues & Parents

It would be a mistake to assume that when it comes to the topic of human connection, successful teaching is solely a matter of cultivating excellent teacher-student relationships. Although this can make a huge difference in terms of students' learning, it is not the whole story. There are teachers who perform well in the classroom, cultivating amicable and productive working relationships with students. Unfortunately, some of these same teachers can be unhelpful colleagues or unapproachable for parents. In the bigger picture, poor working relationships within teams, or with parents, can damage, or at the very least, limit the effectiveness of teaching and learning in a school.

Alongside successful behaviour management strategies, it helps greatly if you can effectively manage human connections with challenging colleagues and tricky parents. In some ways, this subsection can be viewed as an extension of the last subsection about behaviour management because it is about dealing with difficult individuals one to one. If you have not read the Effective Behaviour Management subsection, I recommend you do so because many of the same principles apply. I focus this subsection specifically on interactions with non-student members of the school community and what you can do to enrich those relationships – especially for those occasions when there are conflicts of interest. If you are in a school leadership position, you will find the advice here to be even more relevant.

After you have mastered your own emotional state, the most important point that I would emphasise is the importance of being able to listen. The act of listening itself is often the first step in the process of engaging in interpersonal mindfulness (an important component of emotional mastery – to be discussed in more detail later on in this book). By listening intensely, you show a sincere desire to understand what the other person, be that colleague or parent, is experiencing. Far from being a passive activity, listening is one of the most active things you can do. Sometimes I find that people simply need to vent – and by listening well, you can accurately gauge the situation while helping the other person to sound out their thoughts and feelings.

It might come as a surprise, but there is a lot we can learn from field-tested negotiation techniques used in hostage situations. This is because, whenever difficult confrontations arise in the school context, which they almost certainly will from time to time, the same principles and techniques used in hostage negotiations apply to dealing with tricky parents or disgruntled colleagues.

According to psychotherapy research, when individuals feel they are being listened to, they tend to listen to themselves more carefully. In addition, according to former hostage negotiator, Chris Voss (2016), they tend to become less defensive, demonstrating more effort to listen to others' points of view. In situations where there is a potential for disagreement, instead of prioritising your argument, make your only focus the other person and what they have to say. Listening attentively goes a long way to diffusing a potential conflict.

As with students, the tone you choose can be a powerful tool. You can be direct as long as you create a feeling of safety by validating the other person's emotions and speaking in a calm tone. Chris Voss refers to such a voice as the "Late-Night FM DJ Voice".

Mirroring can also be an effective technique. Mirroring is a phenomenon that follows a very profound biological principle: we fear what is different and are attracted to what is similar. Mirroring of the other person's speech, body language, vocabulary and tone of voice when practised consciously, is the art of insinuating similarity. It might seem odd to apply such negotiation techniques (taken from hostage situations no less) to the school context. Nevertheless, it is only by using and applying such techniques that adequate trust and safety can be created and productive conversations can begin.

It is a cliché to say that you cannot make everyone happy. This is especially true in a school context where there are so many competing priorities and diverse sets of interests. Sometimes in any position of responsibility it is necessary to say no, hold your ground and diffuse the conflicts of interest which invariably arise. In addition to the aforementioned techniques, I have found it to be extremely helpful to validate the feelings of the other person. Consider the following example from my exchange of emails with a parent unhappy about her son's placement in a new class:

Dear Mr. Will,

I am writing to express our disappointment with Toby's new class.

He did not stay with any of the friends I told you about before, and to make it worse, they all stayed together in another class. I don't know how it could get any worse than that.

He will be with no friends.

He put Michael's name to make up the pizza and will be with him. But he is not a friend.

We are really sorry about it as you were aware of Toby's situation.

I will ask again for your attention to take care of him at the beginning of the year and to make any change if needed. Maybe it is still possible for him to change for the other desired class.

As the beginning of the classes approaches he is getting more worried about it.

Best,

Liz

....

Dear Ms Liz,

Thank you for your email.

First of all, I am very sorry to hear that you and Toby feel disappointment with Toby's new class. I do appreciate though, you taking the time to share your concerns with me.

It can be a worrisome time for many students before the start of a new school year, especially those students like Toby who are not entirely happy with the class mixing. As a year group, we do our best to take into consideration every child's needs and preferences. Unfortunately, with so many constraints and variables involved with the class mixing process, it is not always possible to get every student's ideal class mix.

That being said, the start of every new academic year is an opportunity for all students to begin afresh both academically and socially. Nevertheless, I have cc'd the Class 5 Coordinator, Ms Jennifer and Tutor of Class 5G, Ms Angela into this email, so that they are also aware of your concerns. We will keep a close eye on Toby, working together to ensure that he is well taken care of and forms a congenial relationship with his new peers, especially at the beginning of the year.

Please do rest assured that every effort will be made to make sure that Toby has a positive start to the year in his new class. I hope this email helps to put your minds at rest, but if you do have any further concerns as the year progresses, please do not hesitate to get in touch.

Best wishes,

Mr Will

....

Hello Mr. Will,

Toby was feeling very sad today. He said he does not have any friends to talk to in his new class. He was crying and it is hard to see him like this. Everything is so different for him and he is with none of his friends from last year.

I am very disappointed. Last year was hard for him with us getting separated and I let the school know how difficult things have been. This year is not going to be easy.

I still can't understand the class division, as we talked about it and you said I could feel relieved because Toby would quickly make friends in his new class. This has not happened, and none of his few friends that I sent you in a list are with him. And all of them are together in another class. None of his actual peers in his new class are even close to being his friend. I have never felt so disappointed with a decision made by the school. It is hard to understand.

The same thing happened to my other son. At that time, they called the class that had all the friends together as the "dream class", and I prefer not to say how they called the other two classes. He is still struggling with it as the ones that are together make the programs together and they don't ever invite him.

I strongly suggest the school does not do things like this. When you put together 5 friends and one stays out, it is really hard on the one who is left out.

With Toby, I was worried before the division and I let the school know. I let you know.

I am very worried. I really don't know what to do.

Liz

....

Dear Liz,

Thank you for reaching out to us. I am sorry to hear about how you and Toby have been feeling, and we will do our best to address this issue.

The start of a new academic year, especially moving from Primary to Secondary can be a challenging transition for some students. Toby's emotional wellbeing is very important to us, and he should feel comfortable in school.

I will talk to Toby and Ms Jennifer/Ms Angela on Monday, so that we can discuss with Toby his feelings in more depth. Please do encourage Toby to be open and honest with us. We will find an appropriate solution together, while hopefully empowering Toby to feel involved in this process.

I will contact you again after Monday, to let you know the outcome from our conversations with Toby, and how we will go forward from here.

Kind regards,

Mr Will

After the follow-up:

Dear Liz,

Ms Jennifer, Ms Angela and I have now all met to talk about Toby's class. Toby and I have also had a meeting to talk to our school psychologist, Ms Jane earlier today (cc'd in this email).

I have discussed in more detail with Toby the decision process behind him going into Class 5G. Toby has explained to us his feelings, and we have been discussing practical solutions to help overcome these initial doubts. Ms Jennifer has also made some useful observations, which she would like to discuss with you.

In the meantime, the best approach would be for Toby to build new friendships in his current class. As I explained to Toby, his new class is made up of particularly kind and caring children – and he is very unlikely to experience the sort of problems that he had last year with his new peers. Additionally, we have organised (with Toby's active participation), a new buddy from Class 5G, Michael McNulty. Michael is very keen to build a friendship with Toby – and I would even encourage them to meet for play dates (outside of school, if possible). Toby's seating arrangement will be changed, to make sure that he is seated near Michael.

Toby feels relieved now that he understands better the reasons for this class mix and the new friendships this can bring about.

Ms Jennifer will be contacting you shortly. Please do also meet with Ms Angela, who has important information to share with you regarding Toby.

Best wishes,

Mr Will

....

Hello Mr Will,

I just saw Toby and he feels relieved.

Let's see how it goes. Hope he feels happy soon!

Thank you for your support.

Liz

....

The topics about which that parents or fellow colleagues complain can vary wildly. The purpose of sharing this email exchange has been to highlight several principles that will always apply whenever you are faced with a situation in which you cannot meet the other person's demands either because of school policy or some other complicating circumstance. First and foremost, it is important to remember that in many cases, when someone first appears to be particularly upset or obstinate about disagreeing with a "school decision" there are other emotional issues going on in the background. You should never take anything personally if judgements are being levied at you.

Parents, especially, can sometimes transfer their frustrations (which are completely unrelated to school) onto their child's teacher, channelling and projecting a small, school-related problem, making it much bigger than it ought to be. These feelings invariably are projected onto the child, which only serves to perpetuate the problem.

In such situations, you should allow the person to vent, validating their emotions as they do so. It is important to explain your position calmly, clearly and politely – while highlighting all the strategies that you can initiate to mitigate the other person's problems. Oftentimes such strategies will involve you working in teams to provide a network of support for the child, the parent and yourself. Every case is different of course. What I would like to emphasise though, is that dealing with the irksome or contentious situations involving people is a skill – and just like any skill, it will improve with practice.

10. Cultivating a Growth Mindset

I have already mentioned the importance of monitoring your internal monologue and inner voice to ensure positive and affirming self-talk. As well as having an impact on your emotional state, which influences behaviour in the classroom for better or worse, it greatly affects your mindset.

Mindset refers to the assumptions and expectations you have for yourself and others, which determine your commitment to any given task. Dr Carol Dweck (2007), author of *Mindset: The New Psychology of Success*, came up with the terms 'fixed mindset' and 'growth mindset' to describe the intrinsic beliefs people have about learning and intelligence. Learners with a fixed mindset believe there is a limit on how much they can learn and develop intellectually. Those with a growth mindset, on the other hand, believe that they can develop their talents and abilities through effort.

Although individuals may not necessarily be aware of their mindset, it can still be identified based on their behaviour. The mindset of an individual becomes particularly evident in the face of setbacks or failures. A student with a fixed mindset dreads failure, because it is a negative statement on his or her basic abilities, whereas individuals with a growth-mindset do not worry so much about failure, since they realise their performance and learning can be improved.

As educators, we must do all that we can to cultivate our growth mindset first. This means we should be lifelong learners, keen to develop our skills and acquire new ones. After all we are role models for one another and for the students we teach, and to have a growth mindset also shows our students we believe they can be successful. Equipped with a growth mindset, educators will adapt their teaching style and instructional material to ensure all students can learn.

Recent advances in neuroscience have shown that the brain is much more malleable than previously thought (Willingham, 2009). Research on brain plasticity shows how the connectivity between neurons changes with experience. With ongoing practice, neural networks grow new connections, strengthen existing ones, and build insulation that speeds the transmission of impulses. Teaching learners about their brain plasticity helps to shift mindsets from fixed to growth, which then leads to increased motivation and achievement.

In addition to teaching about brain plasticity, the type of feedback teachers give to students can have a huge impact on their mindset. For example, studies presented by Dweck have shown that telling children they are intelligent encourages a fixed mindset, whereas praising effort cultivates a growth mindset. Positive language through praise of effort (e.g., "you must have worked hard on this task") has proven to be more productive than praise of ability (e.g., "you must be clever at doing this task"). Results from Dweck's research has shown that students praised for ability on a task were much less successful on subsequent tasks than those praised for their effort. When students have a growth mindset, they develop their grit and resilience. In other words, they are more likely to take on new challenges, persevere when the going gets tough and learn from setbacks, which all serves to increase their abilities and achievement.

According to Hattie & Clark (2019), errors, not knowing and misconceptions are the occasions when a growth mindset thinking is most powerful. In Part Three, we look at the sort of feedback teachers should provide as part of their teaching strategy in order to cultivate students' growth mindset, which makes all the difference for learning.

11. Mindfulness

A related idea to growth mindset is that of mindfulness. By its nature, mindfulness practice can help to break the pattern of habitual, self-limiting, and 'fixed' mindsets about our students and ourselves. I certainly believe that mindfulness can serve as an effective tool for helping us to take control of our inner voice while also helping us to master our emotions. In the bigger picture, mindfulness practices such as relaxation techniques and breathing exercises can help to foster human connection.

There are a vast array of mindfulness interventions and initiatives around the world in education. Some notable examples include the 'Mindfulness in Schools Project', 'Mindful Schools', 'MindUP' and 'Smiling Mind'. At the time of writing, mindfulness has been introduced as an official subject in several hundred schools in England in an effort to teach children about the importance of looking after their mental health.

These moves reflect recognition of the fact that mindfulness practice can be an important part of successful teaching as well as the overall health of students. Recent scientific advances, for instance, allow us to see that the parts of the brain associated with positive emotions like happiness, empathy and compassion actually become stronger and more active as people engage in mindfulness practice (Williams et al., 2001). Studies also show that mindfulness helps us with the regulation of emotion, attention, thought and behaviour (Jennings & Siegel, 2015). Happiness is an important prerequisite to ensure both successful teaching and learning takes place.

However, I am aware that there exists some confusion related to mindfulness which I would like to clear up. Mindfulness can be confused with meditation and while there certainly is overlap between the two terms, there are some important differences as well.

According to the authors of *Mindfulness – A practical guide to finding peace in a*

64

frantic world, Mark Williams and Danny Penman state:

'Mindfulness is about observation without criticism; being compassionate with yourself…
In essence, mindfulness allows you to catch negative thought patterns before they tip you
into a downward spiral. It begins the process of putting you back in control of your life.'
(Williams & Penman, 2011, pp. 5)

In other words, mindfulness is both the state of mastering emotions and
the tool to achieve this mastery. As a form of meditation, mindfulness is
about focusing on being in the present, such as focusing completely on
eating soup, taking in its scent, warmth and taste and letting go of unwanted
emotions from your mind in the process. In this way, you are monitoring,
in real time, your experience of taste and doing so in a nonjudgmental way.
This is an excellent and much needed practice. A major study into mental
wellbeing conducted by the University of Harvard in 2010 for example,
found that people spend almost half of their time (46.9%) thinking about
something other than what they are actually doing.[5] Certainly, neither
successful teaching nor learning can take place if the teacher is not rooted
to the present moment.

My personal journey and understanding of mindfulness began back in 2009,
when I went to northern India on a 10-day silent meditation retreat. Up
until that point, I had become accustomed to distraction. On my retreat, all
that distraction was quite literally taken away – no mobile phone, no one to
talk to, no reading material – literally nothing to do except attend scheduled
meal and meditation times. The experience was arduous; even by the end I
never really felt that I had been able to meditate successfully. Instead, I
would just close my eyes, try to concentrate on my breath and be
bombarded with thoughts darting back and forth – thoughts about the past
and thoughts about the future. I could not escape them. When the 10 days
were finally up, I felt it had all been a waste of time and I had achieved
nothing more than a disdain for meditation.

Since then, however, I have gained a new understanding of this experience.
I realise just how limiting our thoughts can be. Most of us, most of the
time are operating unconsciously on autopilot; our minds flit from one
thought to the next like hummingbirds. As Williams and Pennman (2011,
p. 9) explain, when we feel even a little unhappy, our thoughts rush in,
trawling through memories to find those that echo our emotional state.
This can draw us into an emotional quicksand because our state of mind is
intimately connected with memory. One thought or feeling triggers the

---

[5] http://www.danielgilbert.com/KILLINGSWORTH%20&%20GILBERT%20(2010).pdf

next, and then the next. Before long, the original thought – no matter how fleeting – has gathered up a raft of similar thoughts and you have become lost in a particular feeling.

Some years later, in 2012, I discovered – without realising it at the time – mindfulness as meditation. I had embarked on the Camino de Santiago, a long pilgrim route stretching across Spain to the town of Santiago de Compostella. Over the space of a couple of weeks, I walked almost 200 miles. Unaccustomed to such long walks, my feet quickly became covered with blisters, and, upon my arrival at Santiago, I had tendonitis in both ankles. I did, however, love the experience. During those long walks, I would get into a rhythm and become acutely aware of my surroundings, including the sights, sounds and smells of the experience. In other words, I was experiencing the very essence of mindfulness meditation.

The state that I had unsuccessfully been trying to reach through meditation in India was a state of mindfulness. While mindfulness is involved in most forms of meditation, mindfulness is itself a form of meditation, which simply requires you to remain aware and present in the moment. Rather than ruminating on the past or obsessing about the future, mindfulness encourages awareness of your present surroundings – as I experienced on the Camino de Santiago. In a state of mindfulness, we are no longer operating on autopilot and instead have a space of mind that gives us the ability to pause before reacting mindlessly. The beauty of mindfulness, however, is that it is something we can practice almost anywhere – including in the classroom.

If a teacher is not mindful of what they are doing, the classroom environment can be a setup for stress-related health problems:

Under pressure, some students become disruptive, distracted, and even defiant, and teachers may become anxious, frustrated, embarrassed, and hopeless. From this perspective, it's easy to see why teachers are burning out and students aren't learning. The stress response is derailing our teaching and students' learning.

The idea of applying a mindfulness-based approach to supporting teachers' well-being make perfect sense. Furthermore, if we could give teachers the skills to better manage these social and emotional demands, the classroom climate would improve and so would student behavior and learning. (Jennings and Siegel, 2015, xix)

Mindfulness has not only been shown to benefit social relationships (Karremans et al., 2017), but it can also be practised specifically in the context of social relationships (Kok and Singer, 2017). Being mindful while interacting facilitates effective communication (Burgoon et al. 2000).

Specifically, this is known as interpersonal mindfulness. According to Jennings and Siegel (2015, pp. 6-7), interpersonal mindfulness involves the development and practice of the following behaviours:

- Listening with full attention to others;

- Present-centred awareness of emotions experienced by oneself and others during interactions;

- Openness to, acceptance of, and receptivity to others' thoughts and feelings;

- Self-regulation: low emotional and behavioural reactivity and low automaticity in reaction to the everyday behaviours of others;

- Compassion for oneself and others

It is not difficult to see how such qualities can be invaluable to the school context. When we encounter a disruptive child, an enraged parent or an obnoxious colleague, we can sense and observe our own emotional states without becoming reactive or impulsive. In this way, we achieve a state of equanimity and are in a much better position to teach successfully, as our ability to handle difficult situations improve.

For further information and practical exercises to develop your mindfulness practice, I highly recommend 'Mindfulness for Teachers' by internationally recognised leader in the field, Patricia Jennings.

12. Provide Meaningful Feedback for Teachers

For educational leaders, cultivating a growth mindset for students and staff should go hand in hand with creating a culture of positive and meaningful feedback. According to Sam Goldstein, author of *Understanding and Managing Children's Classroom Behavior: Creating Sustainable, Resilient Classrooms,* effective educational leaders model and frame evaluation as an instrument or tool to support the staff's growth.

People all have blind spots. Nobody can really see himself or herself objectively, and for this reason, it is everyone's responsibility to help others learn what is true about them, by giving them honest feedback. In particular, it is imperative that staff receive specific feedback regarding the area in which they want and need growth to be more effective educators. If leaders model this consistently, teachers will carry this practice back into their classrooms. As Benjamin Bloom (1984, pp. 11) explains:

When teachers are helped to secure a more accurate picture of their own teaching methods and styles of interaction with their students, they will increasingly be able to provide more favorable learning conditions for more of their students.

It might sound obvious, but as an educational leader, it is nonetheless important to remember that teachers do have an emotional attachment to being observed and evaluated. Leaders must focus on the growth of their teachers whilst keeping the relationship positive. It becomes invaluable then to have emotional intelligence, to coach staff whilst being mindful of each individual's personality, interests and areas for growth. Just as it is important to praise children, it is equally important for teachers to be praised. When lessons do not go as planned, feedback should be presented positively, focusing on what went well before outlining strategies for improvement.

Over the next several pages, I have included three examples of lesson observations. Names and other key details have been changed to protect the confidentiality of the teachers and students observed. The observation template used is not so important – these can come in all different shapes and sizes. What is important is that the feedback given is positive, detailed and provides actionable pointers for how the teacher can improve. In addition, you will notice several distinct features of this written feedback:

1. *Photos have been included.* I recommend the use of photos, because they will help to remind both you (the observer) and the teacher about key details of the lesson.

2. *Links to video can be useful.* For most of my observations, I film the teacher's lesson. As well as helping to remind both the observer and teacher about key details of the lesson, video serves to make the lesson observation notes more engaging and memorable. Video also serves to help elicit more realistic self-feedback from the teacher.

3. *There is a 'Focus of Observation' section at the beginning.* It helps for every lesson observation to have a particular focus, which will vary according to the area that the teacher needs to develop his or her classroom practice.

4. *A summary of each key aspect of the lesson should be given*, e.g. 'Teaching/Planning', 'Learning', 'Assessment', 'Classroom Management', etc. In particular, irrespective of the observation focus, there is an emphasis in all the feedback on what students are actually learning.

5. *An EBI (Even Better If) section*, which outlines key actionable pointers for the teacher to improve.

As a side note, one of the best ways teachers can improve their practice after feedback, is to observe those who have already integrated feedback into their practice. If a particular teacher has an issue with differentiation for example, it can be invaluable for her to observe a teacher who excels in this area. This is because:

Principles are powerful but cases are memorable. Only in the continued interaction between principles and cases can practitioners and their mentors avoid the inherent limitations of theory-without-practice or the equally serious restrictions of vivid practice without the mirror of principle. (Shulman, 1996, cited in Darling-Hammond et al., 2005, pp. 430)

Lesson Observation 1

Observer: Will Fastiggi	Class: 3E	Date:
Teacher: Ms Judith		
Subject: Social Studies	Learning Objective: To analyse qualities of a leader	

Focus of Observation: The use of Seesaw app to collect evidence of, showcase and provide feedback on students' work.

PLANNING /TEACHING   Evidence/Comments

objectives appropriate and communicated clearly	You began this lesson by giving the children very clear instructions about what they needed to do and then congratulating them for being settled. This positive approach continued throughout your lesson and helped to facilitate a productive learning environment.
evidence of differentiation	
lesson appropriately structured, with assessment opportunities identified	
designs effective learning sequences	
good subject knowledge	
purposeful, paced and focused	
clear instructions and appropriate vocabulary	This lesson was also well paced. You provided an engaging warm up activity, which involved the children watching a video of Megan Markle speaking, and then asking them to describe her. While the video was playing, you made effective use of the time by going around the classroom, to help ensure all children were logged into their Seesaw accounts.
a range of teaching strategies are used: modelling, role play, demonstrating, partner talk	
a range of questions	

used; open/closed, differentiated	
questions target individuals	
high expectations are shared	

On Seesaw you had set them the 3-minute assignment: 'What words would you use to describe this champion for change?' Meanwhile, you made effective use of the Class Dojo stopwatch, to ensure everyone was on track. It was good to see that all the children quickly got on with this task. I noticed however, that Michael spent all of this time drawing a picture on the iPad of Megan Markle rather than writing any words. Perhaps a more relevant activity for Michael (if writing is a problem) would be to select relevant adjectives from a pack of word cards to then be photographed and uploaded onto the app. Alternatively, would it be possible to differentiate the activities on the SeeSaw app itself? For example, for children who have issues writing quickly, could you use some kind of digital writing frame?

LEARNING   Evidence/Comments

pupils fully engaged with the lesson, are interested, experiment and take risks	Your use of routines such as "Ninja Mode" (for partner whisper noise level) were well embedded into the lesson, helping to facilitate an appropriate environment for students' learning.
pupils apply thinking and learning skills, independence and responsibility	
tasks are appropriately	

differentiated
tasks challenge pupils to think for themselves
high level of pupil participation
variety of opportunity for pupils to explain/watch/listen /ask questions and discuss
pupils show independent learning skills
pupils sustain concentration, work productively and achieve their potential
pupils inspired to produce their best work

The lesson had a variety of opportunities for children to explain, watch, listen, answer questions and ask questions. After listening to the audio clip which described a famous leader for instance, you used your "magic pot" to select students at random, to ask questions about what they wanted to know. After revealing that the leader being described in the audio clip was in fact Adolf Hitler, you then gave students time to think-pair-share. This activity moved smoothly into explaining the learning intention - "today we are going to look at what makes a good leader."

You linked to children's previous learning: "I was so impressed by your philosophical discussion last time, I thought, why don't we have one today?" Points of transition such as these could be good opportunities to make the language of knowledge, skills and understanding more explicit.

The Concept Frequency Graph was a great medium to collate all the children's philosophical questions and then share these as part of your mini-plenary.

It was great to see you deliver a session of P4C (Philosophy for Children). There was lots of discussion in this lesson, which lent itself well to reinforcing and developing students' speaking and listening skills as well as fostering enquiry-based learning. They have also clearly learnt to begin creating their own philosophical questions.

As a facilitator of P4C, I particularly liked the fact that, when inviting a child to contribute an answer in front of the other children, you were careful to repeat the answer back, paraphrasing, clarifying and developing this answer, to help the other students understand, when necessary.

ENGLISH   Evidence/Comments

English spoken and/or read confidently and correctly	English was widely spoken throughout the lesson, and you consistently used a range of positive behaviour management strategies, to ensure children would keep this up.
writing on board or flip chart grammatically accurate and spelt correctly	

ASSESSMENT   Evidence/Comments

prior knowledge activated	All of the activities linked back to the main focus of the lesson to identify what makes a good leader. Prior knowledge was evidently drawn upon, for example, when children discussed Adolf Hitler.
relates back to learning objectives/success criteria	
learning styles catered for	
plenary drew together what had been learned	
feedback to children in a timely, constructive manner	The use of peer-to-peer communication

	through both think-pair-share (Ninja mode) talk and group discussion effectively served assessment for learning. You also asked a range of open questions to elicit children's understanding throughout the lesson. Your mini-plenaries (e.g. using the Concept Frequency Graph) and circle time discussion were all successful in terms of both assessing children's understanding and drawing together their learning.
monitor progress	
misconceptions addressed	
	For the activities set via the Seesaw platform, it could have been useful to share an example of a child's submitted work to display on the interactive whiteboard. Whilst having this student's work on display, it would provide a good assessment for learning opportunity, as you can elicit from the other children any misconceptions, what they think the child has done well and what could be developed. You could also use such an opportunity to model how you give feedback via the Seesaw platform.
	How do you currently give feedback via the Seesaw app? Is there a way that these portfolios, including your feedback, could be shared as links on a spreadsheet? Being able to share these portfolios would be useful for showcasing students' work, helping to develop teaching practice and moderating feedback and marking.

CLASSROOM MANAGEMENT   Evidence/ Comments

other adults, where present, give active support	Your classroom clearly has a culture in which high standards of behaviour are expected and a good variety of strategies are used. You have cultivated an atmosphere in the classroom that is very conducive to learning.
high standards of behaviour are insisted upon and a range of strategies used	
good behaviour is, praised and encouraged	After the video and at all other points of transition in the lesson, I was impressed to see

appropriate action is taken to promote self-control and independence	how effectively you kept the children's attention using a range of different strategies, e.g. Class Dojo, praise, countdowns, class points, mantras ("Stop.. wait a minute.. shhh").
the atmosphere in the classroom is conducive to learning	
resources, including new technology, are ready and available for the task	For example, you were quick to recognise, praise and reward children for paying attention: "First of all, I have to give you all 50 points because I saw nobody touching their devices." You made sure to regularly praise individual children at several opportunities, e.g. "Pablo, I love how you're showing you're listening – reward to give."

When children were distracted, you were quick to take appropriate action without it slowing down your lesson: "Michael, that's your final warning – put your iPad face down." Likewise, you were always careful to help guide the children to appropriate actions without being overly negative: "Oh, it's a shame I can hear Portuguese. I really would love to hear English."

You modelled manners and politeness throughout the lesson, regularly using please and thank you, e.g. "Elizabeth, you may now please turn off the lights."

The combination of your behaviour management strategies and overall teaching manner have enabled you to build an excellent rapport with the children in your class – well done!

Comments

Thank you, Judith, for inviting me to observe this excellent lesson, which demonstrated elements of enquiry-based learning and the development of children's philosophical understanding about the qualities of a leader through P4C (Philosophy for Children). You successfully employed many different tools and strategies, to maintain high standards of student behaviour, engagement and participation. In particular, you have embedded learning technologies effectively, namely Class Dojo and the Seesaw app, to support teaching and learning. The strong emphasis on student collaboration and discussion clearly demonstrated new learning having taken place during the lesson. You confidently supported all the children in their thinking, reasoning and questioning, as well as facilitating an efficient dialogue in the way children spoke and listened to one another. Students were challenged to think critically about what makes an effective leader and to justify their ideas with explanations. Your lesson had a good pace, and along with your calm, fair and consistent manner, you cultivated an atmosphere that was very conducive for student learning.

EBI (Even Better If):

- Make explicit the language of Knowledge, Skills and Understanding during the lesson. E.g. "we are demonstrating for this task our knowledge of the ways in which Megan Markle is a champion for change."
- A skill rubric on display (according to the key history skill 3.11 for this unit) would be useful. Take a look again at the one we looked at last week in our staff development session.
- Whilst students can record their voices using the Seesaw app, please just make the different options explicit before setting children off on their task.
- Display an example of students' work on the interactive whiteboard, to help guide students' discussion and model how you would provide feedback, to encourage students to follow the same approach when giving each other feedback.
- Share Ms Judith's Seesaw app access with Will.
- At transition points in your teacher instruction, you used "OK" fairly frequently – try to think of different words instead of using "OK".

Lesson Observation 2

Observer: Will Fastiggi	Class: 5A	Date:
Teacher: Isabel		
Subject: Science	**Learning Objective:** To classify animals	

Focus of Observation: Challenge and facilitation of enquiry-based learning

PLANNING /TEACHING · Evidence/Comments

objectives appropriate and communicated clearly	You began this lesson by recapping on students' previous learning, using a snippet of video some students had already produced. This was a great start, and you used the opportunity to go over key
evidence of differentiation	vocabulary: "taxonomy", "six kingdoms", "species". After the video, you also reminded students of other
lesson appropriately structured, with assessment opportunities identified	points, e.g. "I've chosen Tony and George's mind map because it's got an explanation of what you learnt…"
designs effective learning sequences	
good subject knowledge	
purposeful, paced and focused	
clear instructions and appropriate vocabulary	You then gave out post-it notes for the students to write down things they already know about the topic. This would have been a good opportunity for a
a range of teaching strategies are	brief "think-pair-share" to promote peer assessment

used: modelling, role play, demonstrating, partner talk	and collaboration. All children were on task though, and you provided plenty of opportunities for them to share their thoughts and ideas.
a range of questions used; open/closed, differentiated	
questions target individuals	
high expectations are shared	
	Your teaching demonstrated a positive rapport with the students, and you have clearly established a productive working environment in your classroom, which is conducive for student learning. I particularly liked the way you used praise and encouragement when listening to the students' ideas about what they would like to know.
	Just be careful to ensure that when a student responds to one of your questions, you repeat, and if necessary, paraphrase this response back, so that everyone has heard what the student has just said. For example, some students speak quietly and I was not able to hear what they had said. This may have been the case for some students in the classroom too.
	The sequence of the lesson was excellent, as you seamlessly facilitated transitions from one activity to another, which was pacey and kept the students on track.

You put images on display of several different animals and used these as a prompt for eliciting the students' knowledge of vertebrates versus invertebrates.

You kept your questions open, helping to cultivate enquiry-based learning. Two of the questions, "What do you think?" and "What do you wonder?" then served as posters, which, using post-it notes collated all the children's responses. You skillfully allocated different tasks around the room: "This poster is going to walk around" (while collecting student post-its) and meanwhile, you assigned another group the task of writing everything they knew about vertebrates and invertebrates.

Once you had the posters on display, you used this as an opportunity for a mini-plenary, to discuss the children's key ideas. This provided a great opportunity for the students to demonstrate their knowledge and understanding. At all times, you were careful to facilitate the children's enquiry rather than dispense information. It was also good to see you make use of the Class Dojo stopwatch, which you kept visible, to help manage the students' time and keep everyone on task.

LEARNING	Evidence/Comments
pupils fully engaged with the lesson, are interested, experiment and take risks	You reminded the students of key facts and used a range of questions to elicit the students' knowledge and understanding: "The animal kingdom is divided into two main groups: vertebrates and invertebrates. Each group has further subgroups…. What are the five classes?"
pupils apply thinking and learning skills, independence and responsibility	
tasks are appropriately differentiated	You also fostered curiosity by asking questions that were both challenging and interesting: "Do we have more vertebrates or invertebrates?"
tasks challenge pupils to think for themselves	I was impressed with how you scaffolded your questions, guiding the students to the correct answers and helping to elicit key vocabulary:
high level of pupil participation	"They have different what? … Why can't we put

variety of opportunity for pupils to explain/watch/listen/ask questions and discuss	them in the same group? … They have different characteristics!"
pupils show independent learning skills	
pupils sustain concentration, work productively and achieve their potential	
pupils inspired to produce their best work	

For the main activity, students were organised into two large working groups — one working on a task about vertebrates, the other task about invertebrates. You maintained high expectations throughout: "You will be working as a big group, so try not to talk too much."

You moved around the classroom, supporting and challenging students, as necessary.

You set the students an assignment via BrainPOP. This worked well and the students were engaged with their activities. I would just recommend that you ask children to bring in their earphones for these activities, so they can listen to the videos without the noise interrupting others.

ENGLISH   Evidence/Comments

English spoken and/or read confidently and correctly	All children were speaking in English and were able to confidently articulate what they were learning – both when speaking and
writing on board or flip chart grammatically accurate and spelt correctly	writing. Well done!

ASSESSMENT   Evidence/Comments

prior knowledge activated	In addition to the range of questions you used
relates back to learning objectives/success criteria	throughout the lesson, you used the plenary to draw together what had been learnt during the
learning styles catered for	lesson. You then used this time to correct a fundamental misconception: "Let's look at
plenary drew together what had been learned	what you said about there being more vertebrates than invertebrates." After
feedback to children in a timely, constructive manner	correcting the misconception, it was great to see you end the lesson with a hook: "In the
monitor progress	

82

	afternoon, we're going to find out why."
misconceptions addressed	

CLASSROOM MANAGEMENT   Evidence/Comments

other adults, where present, give active support	You regularly used a countdown "3 - 2 - 1", which worked well to get the children's attention. When you saw a child not paying attention, you were quick to politely address this: "Could you please listen to Adam?"
high standards of behaviour are insisted upon and a range of strategies used	
good behaviour is, praised and encouraged	Just make sure that everyone stops what they are doing, either when you are speaking or when another child is addressing the class, e.g. say: "Pens down, eyes on me." There were several occasions, for example, when I noticed Ian reading his book, either when you were talking or during another activity. Nevertheless, you have clearly established high standards of behaviour, and the students worked very well together.
appropriate action is taken to promote self-control and independence	
the atmosphere in the classroom is conducive to learning	
resources, including new technology, are ready and available for the task	

Comments

This was a fantastic lesson in terms of enquiry-based learning and fostering curiosity on the part of the students. I was particularly impressed by your classroom management and how you skillfully transitioned the children from one activity to another. You have clearly established high expectations for behaviour, and this was evident from how the students were able to work collaboratively in different group formations.   You have also embraced and made excellent use of different technologies such as BrainPOP and Class Dojo, to both facilitate your classroom management and enhance student learning. Bringing all of these elements together, this was a very strong IPC lesson, which kept the students engaged and led to new learning being demonstrated.

EBI (Even better if):

- Students come prepared with earphones/headphones for

watching videos on the Chromebooks/iPads. This will help to minimise unnecessary noise.

- When a student responds to one of your questions, make sure that you repeat, and if necessary, paraphrase this response back, to ensure that everyone has heard what the student has just said.
- Make sure that all students put their pencils, etc. down when you or another student is addressing the class.
- Incorporate opportunities for think-pair-share to promote further collaboration and peer assessment.

Lesson Observation 3

Observer: Will Fastiggi	Class: 4E	Date:
Teacher: Rebecca		
Subject: English	Learning Objective: To define the meaning of key vocabulary	

PLANNING/TEACHING   Evidence/Comments

clear learning objective	The Learning Objective was clearly displayed at the beginning of the lesson and children expected to copy this down into their exercise books.
evidence of differentiation	The success criteria was also visible, but the "Must" criteria was quite difficult to read against the yellow background. Following the traffic light assessment system, keep in mind that 'Must' is red, 'Should' is yellow /orange and 'Could' is green.
lesson appropriately structured, with assessment opportunities identified	
designs effective learning sequences	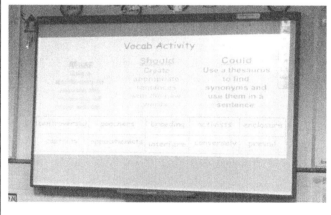
good subject knowledge	
clear instructions and appropriate vocabulary	Lesson was structured well, beginning with a focus on the vocabulary before moving to an example text, which put the vocabulary being studied into context. You showed sound knowledge of word definitions, helping explain to children when they made mistakes or

a range of teaching strategies are used: modelling, role play, demonstrating, partner talk	were unsure. Instructions given to students were clear and concise. However, some mistakes in your use of English grammar were noted (see below). Lesson began with "Around the World" game, which engaged the class and served as a useful introduction.
a range of questions used; open/closed, differentiated	Questions were used effectively to elicit understanding but take care to ensure the grammar is correct, e.g. 'What **does** endangered mean?' *not* 'What endangered means?' 'Did you see…?' *not* 'Did you saw…?'
questions target individuals	When asking children specific questions, it would be useful to repeat the answer given by the child back to the whole class, to make sure everyone hears before making necessary comments and corrections. Planning is succinct, identifying a clear progression of success criteria statements.
high expectations are shared	Effective use was made of the Learning Support Assistant to focus on the lower ability children. In order to make this lesson even better, the actual learning activity should be differentiated rather than differentiating through outcome and support alone. For example, the words could be grouped according to children's ability level with more challenging, less frequently used words (e.g. 'prevail', 'oppositionists') being given to the higher ability learners. Likewise, sentence starter sheets and/or Chromebooks/iPads could be used with the lower ability children. Vary the tone of your voice and occasionally speak a little louder to get (and keep) everyone's attention.

LEARNING   Evidence/Comments

pupils fully engaged with the lesson, are interested, experiment and take risks	Children were engaged in both the game at the beginning and the main activities. There was evidence of new learning taking place during the lesson.
adults engaged with	

	You gave the children lots of opportunities to work collaboratively and share ideas.
play when appropriate	
high level of pupil participation	On the lower ability table it was great to see a time connectives display and key vocabulary sheet.
children with specific learning needs are carefully planned for and supported	
pupils show independent learning skills	
pupils sustain concentration, work productively and achieve their potential	Just take care not
pupils inspired to produce their best work	to put any child on the spot by asking them to read aloud in front of their peers – it's better to ask for volunteers to read aloud.

ENGLISH   Evidence/ Comments

-English positively promoted	All children were talking in English and motivated to complete the tasks set. Dictionaries were made available on tables.
-Classroom environment supports English development *-Children motivated to speak English*	When writing sentences using the whiteboards, several children were not using the words such as 'captivity' and 'prevail' correctly. For example, in the children's examples below, there is a clear misconception that indicates they do not know how to use the present progressive tense to show continuing action. When using the "to be" verb, "I am…" or "My mum is…", the verb 'prevail' needs to end with '-ing' to show continuing action, so the student's sentence should read: 'I am prevailing every football match'. To explain this to the children, you could say something like "Is it correct to say: I am win every football match?" Elicit that they need to use the -ing form of the verb to show continuing

87

action.

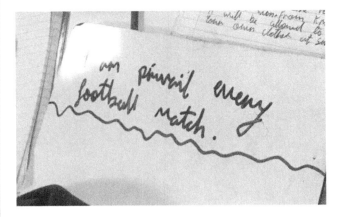

This would have been a good opportunity to have mini-plenaries to address these misconceptions with the whole class. Remember, although a plenary should always feature at the end of a lesson, mini-plenaries can be important part-way through the lesson as well.

ASSESSMENT	**Evidence/ Comments**
prior knowledge activated	Learning of new vocabulary linked to text about zoos.
relates back to learning objectives/ success criteria	Plenary at the end wrapped the lesson up nicely. Be careful though, not to cram in too much. You began talking about sentence starters towards the end of the lesson, which detracted from the main learning focus.
learning styles catered for	You made good use of questioning to both engage and elicit understanding from the students.
plenary drew together what had been learned	I liked the way you used peer assessment, e.g. to "test a friend".
feedback to children in a timely,	Make sure all children have a clear understanding of the definitions for the new vocabulary. Images can be an effective tool to help children remember the definitions. E.g. an image of poachers or an enclosure would be an effective

constructive manner	way of reinforcing your explanations whilst reading the text.
monitor progress	
misconceptions addressed	

CLASSROOM MANAGEMENT   Evidence/ Comments

other adults, where present, give active support	Good classroom management - all children were on task most of the time. Counting down from five worked well.
high standards of behaviour are insisted upon and a range of strategies used	
good behaviour is praised and encouraged	You have a positive rapport with the class and all children were well-behaved during the lesson.
appropriate action is taken to promote self-control and independence	Make sure that after you have counted down from five or said "stop and drop", all children have put pencils down and have their eyes facing you. A couple of children continued to write or were looking away whilst you were talking.
the atmosphere in the classroom is conducive to learning	Consider keeping whiteboard pens in pots on the tables to save you having to give them out in future lessons. Post-it notes can also be invaluable for children to record new vocabulary they learn and then stick on an

resources, including new technology, are ready and available for the task	interactive working wall. Technology (Chromebooks or iPads) would be a useful resource for this type of lesson. Using an online timer can be an excellent way of keeping children on track with each part of the lesson.

Comments

This was a fun and meaningful lesson, which kept the students engaged throughout. You managed the class well, ensuring that students stayed on task and that everyone participated. It is clear that you have developed a strong rapport with your class and you have created a classroom environment, which is conducive to learning. It was also evident by the end of the lesson that new learning had taken place and children had a much better understanding of the topic. I also noticed:

- Both your planning and learning focus were clear and concise.
- The game at the beginning was an excellent introduction and kept the children engaged.
- You have a calm teaching approach, demonstrating a good rapport with the class and all children were well behaved during the lesson.
- You demonstrated good subject knowledge.
- The children were given lots of opportunities to work together to collaborate and share ideas.

Even Better If (EBI):

- Make sure you pick up on misconceptions (e.g. written on the children's whiteboards) during the lesson. Use these as opportunities to deliver a mini-plenary.
- Differentiate the learning activities using sentence starters and technology.
- To get all children's attention, vary your tone of voice and make sure everyone has put their pencils down. This is an excellent TED video to watch about using the power of your voice for lesson delivery:
  https://www.youtube.com/watch?v=H3ddrbeduoo

Oral feedback

Accompanying lesson observations, oral feedback is potentially the most effective way of providing professional development and learning opportunities. Certainly, the need for effective feedback, especially for developing teachers, is extremely important. In fact, there is an excellent TED talk that Bill Gates gave on the subject: *Teachers need real feedback*. According to Bill Gates, teachers around the world need more effective feedback in order for them to improve their teaching practice.

Effective oral feedback has the following features:

– begins with something positive (a headline) – not *"How do you think it went?"*

– specific

– asks questions to develop understanding – aims for dialogue

– describes behaviours not the person

As a teacher receiving the feedback, you should do the following:

– listen to the feedback carefully before responding

– be careful you fully understand what is being said

– ask questions for clarification and exploration

– seek other opinions rather than relying on one source

– decide what you will do as a result of the feedback

As leaders of teaching colleagues, we need to be particularly aware of using coaching strategies for developing teachers' classroom practice. Following a lesson observation, for example, the questions below help provide effective guidance for the teacher:

1. Did all students achieve the learning objective?

2. How do you know?

3. What will you do about those who didn't?

4. How will you assess and use students' prior knowledge?

5. How did you liaise with your teaching assistant before/during/after the lesson?

6. What can students do now that they couldn't at the start of the lesson?

7. How did you make sure students know their next steps in learning?

8. How did you make sure all students know your high expectations?

9. How did you provide challenge for all your students?

10. Did the students enjoy the lesson and how do you know?

I like these ten questions because they have the power to refocus from problem to solution.

The coaching process to support professional development can be distilled into three stages (based on Gerard Egan's Skilled Helper):

Stage 1 Analysis

Where am I now? What's happening here?

Stage 2 Direction setting

Where do I want to be?

Stage 3 Action planning

How will I get there?

Clearly, asking the right questions is a fundamental technique for guiding the person that you are coaching, so that they can find their own solution. This in itself can be a powerful way of unlocking leadership potential in others. It is not the role of the coach to provide answers or to give advice, but instead to support the development and learning of the professional learner – to inspire self-directed change. In order to develop coaching skills further, it is important to become increasingly committed to:

– understanding one's own learning needs

– reflecting on one's practice

– taking an ever-more active role in one's own learning and the learning of others

– acting on what is learned to improve student learning

Some recommended devices for self-observations

In terms of appropriate technologies for enhancing teaching, I have found that the two most effective video recording devices in which to enhance lesson observations are the Swivl and the Samsung Gear 360.

The **Swivl** is a robotic platform accessory for smartphones and tablets, providing an easy way to capture and share video. Swivl is particularly useful as a self-observation tool for teachers. You simply insert the smartphone or tablet into the swiveling platform and wear or hold a digital marker, which the Swivl robot follows using an infrared signal.

The marker itself also captures audio, so even if the presenter is standing several metres away from the device, the video recorded will still provide crystal clear audio. When the video is completed, you can upload it to the Swivl cloud for viewing online anywhere.

There are many educational applications for this sort of technology. As well as being a great tool for recording presentations for flipped learning, its most powerful application is to enhance teaching.

One of the most useful lesson observations I received early on in my teaching career for example, was when a colleague filmed my lesson. Watching the video afterwards was like no other feedback I had ever received; I could actually see myself as others saw me teach. This "self-observation" was incredibly effective, as I was quickly able to see with my own eyes what I was doing well and what I could improve. The additional benefit of having the Swivl robot of course, is that no human observer is needed to record the video for you – the robot does it all for you, enabling you to get a true sense of what you're like as a teacher.

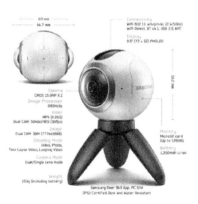

https://www.flickr.com/photos/samsungtomorrow/24859929243

The Samsung Gear 360 is a camera that serves to record a full 360-degree view as video or photo. Once recorded, this technology enables teachers to watch a video of themselves, as well as observe everything that happens in the classroom.

In several lesson observations, I have placed the Gear 360 on a tripod in the middle of the classroom during a lesson. The students then quickly forget that the camera is there, in the middle of the classroom.

As the camera can record everything that is going on around the classroom, it is able to catch many things that can be missed by both the teacher and even the observer such as low-level behaviour issues or students who just need extra support. In this way, the 360-degree video can be incredibly useful and informative as an extra tool for providing teachers with feedback after they have been observed.

After the video has been recorded, it needs to be converted into another format such that you can move around the video (either by dragging the cursor on the screen or using a VR headset), thereby watching in 360-degrees. In other words, the video or photo needs to be stitched from the dual-sphere video into an "equirectangular" (flat mode) video first for it to be viewable in 360-degrees. To transfer into such a format, there is the software that comes with the camera, Gear 360 CyberLink ActionDirector. One thing to keep in mind, however, is that 360-degree videos take up a lot of memory. You therefore need to make sure that you have an SD card with sufficient memory and allow the necessary time for conversion (depending on your computer's processing power, this will probably take about 30-minutes). For these practical reasons, the Gear 360 and similar models, are best used only once in a while, when the extra information provided by the 360-degree panorama needed.

In addition, there are several online options for storing 360-degree images, including:

- 360 player
- Kuula
- Host 360 Photos

The Swivl and Gear 360 cameras are certainly both powerful and easy-to-use tools. By providing teachers with the ability to both film themselves teaching, and at the same time, give teachers a view of themselves from the student's perspective, lesson feedback can become much more thorough. These are tools that I would recommend for any teacher to use, both for watching themselves teach and for watching everything else that has been going on in the classroom while they have been delivering their lesson.

13. Looking for Learning

Teaching and learning are two sides of the same coin; the aim of successful teaching is learning. On the surface of a lesson, a teacher might be well prepared, there can be lots of interactive materials for example, along with engaging activities and questions. However, none of this necessarily equates to student learning. A good practice to get into therefore, is to literally look for learning. The questions on this crib sheet are examples of 'looking for learning'-type questions that can be used with students.

Is there any learning going on?	Is the learning appropriate?
<ul><li>What are you learning?</li><li>What are you learning about?</li><li>What are you learning to do?</li><li>Why are you learning this?</li><li>Are you learning something new or practicing something you already know?</li><li>Are you learning anything new?</li><li>Have you learnt anything new</li></ul>	<ul><li>Is this interesting for you?</li><li>Have you learnt this before?</li><li>How does this build on your previous learning?</li><li>How will this lead onto your next learning?</li><li>How is this connected to your previous learning?</li><li>How is this connected to your next piece of learning?</li></ul>

- today?

- Are you learning stuff that you knew already?

- Are you learning stuff that you could do already?

- What do you know now that you didn't know at the start of the session?

- What can you do now that you couldn't do at the start of the session?

- What do you know now that you didn't know when you came to school this morning?

- Is this difficult for you, easy for you, or is just right?

- What are you going to learn next?

Is the learning sufficient?

- How long have you been doing this?

- Do you have enough time for your learning?

- Do you have too much time?

- Would you like to learn more?

- How do you know if you have been successful in your learning?

- Is this easy learning for you?

- Is this difficult learning for you?

- Is this learning challenging you? Too much? Too little?

- How could this learning be more challenging for you?

What is helping or hindering the learning?

- How do you learn best?

- Does anything stop you learning?

- What does your teacher do to help you learn?

- What do your friends do to help you learn?

- How do you help yourself learn?

- What happens if you get stuck with your learning?

Is the learning engaging?	Any other learning observations?
• Are you enjoying this learning? Why? • What's the most interesting thing you've learned in this work recently? Why? • Are you motivated by this learning? Why? • Do you enjoy learning (in general)? Why/Why not? • What keeps you interested in your learning? Why? • What 'switches you off'? Why? • Do you think it's important to enjoy learning? • Can you describe how you feel when you are enjoying your learning?	

'Looking for Learning' is a leadership toolkit developed by Fieldwork Education, the organisation that created the International Primary Curriculum. It aims to help teachers answer crucial questions such as 'What is learning?' and 'What does it mean to be a learning-focused school?' and helps teachers to improve the learning that is taking place within their classrooms.

You can apply this practice by working with colleagues to see what learning is happening in your classroom. The idea would then be for teachers to visit each other's classrooms to spend up to 20-minutes there, asking the students about their learning. As per the crib sheet, you can have a 'looking for learning' focus, to ascertain for example, if there is learning going on or if the learning is sufficient. You should record the feedback verbatim for later sharing with the teacher.

Having done this process several times, there are several benefits:

1. It can be insightful (and fun) listening to what the students say about their learning.
2. Listening to what students actually think is an effective way to prompt reflection about what is actually happening in the classroom.
3. The information garnered from students can be extremely useful to share with the teachers, and this can serve additional feedback after lesson observations.
4. It is a great way to celebrate the learning that is going on in the classrooms on a daily basis.

14. Leading Teaching & Learning

It is almost impossible to implement successful teaching in a school without leadership. After all, the work of an educator can easily get messy, with interference from demanding parents, behavioural challenges from neglected students and frequent changes in educational initiatives. The role of a school leader therefore, is to ensure that teachers thrive at their job – even when the work gets tough. This can only happen when teachers feel supported, encouraged and inspired by an effective leadership team.

In his book, 'The Human Side of School Change', Robert Evans (1996) makes several excellent points about innovation and leadership:

1. Every educator is a change agent, helping students to learn and grow.

2. Authentic leaders embrace projects that reflect their values and institutional goals. They concentrate on what matters to them. They have definite notions of what is important, and they pay attention to these targets.

3. It is mainly through consistent beliefs and goals expressed in consistent actions that we perceive a leader's integrity. Authentic leaders translate their beliefs and values into concrete actions at a fundamental level.

4. Whether it is challenging thoroughly resistant staff or staying close to students or spending large amounts of time on the job – or exemplifying virtue – authentic leaders embody character in action: they don't just say, they do.

5. Educators want leaders who offer proof or promise of being able to "make things happen", whether this means fixing problems, finding resources, or handling people. These traits build a basic platform without which a leader lacks presence and clout and is not taken seriously.

100

6. All leaders, if they are to be passionate about what they do, need to know what they stand for. According to Evans, this involves exploring one's own values and core beliefs. Most educators in education have values that cluster around two main headings, "equity" and "excellence". Some educators stress the importance of opportunity, fairness, diversity and community. They are likely to promote the idea of "growth mindset" and that "all children can learn". Other educators emphasise goals, challenge, responsibility, and striving. They are more likely to speak of "excellence" and "standards", of bringing out the best in children by measuring them against high benchmarks. Most educators share both these values to some degree, although differences of emphasis can lead to significant differences in the kinds of schools they develop.

7. It's a good habit to reflect on our strengths in order to identify one's core beliefs and values. In doing so, the essence of what matters most to us can be found. These core values should guide our mission as educators and school leaders.

8. It is only by identifying our core beliefs and values that we can be authentic leaders, as we are then able to communicate both to ourselves and others what we stand for.

9. As well as being authentic, research has shown that the most successful leaders of innovation all fulfilled four key roles:

1. Resource provider

2. Instructional resource

3. Communicator

4. Visible presence

Interestingly, each of these roles can be exercised in very different ways whilst still being effective. According to Fullan (1991, pp. 158), some leaders are "strong, aggressive, fearless", others "quiet, nurturing, supportive". The most successful leaders are "not human chameleons, but…people of distinctive personalities who behave consistently in accordance with that personality" (Badaracco and Ellsworth, 1989, pp. 208).

10. Leaders' greatest assets are "their own passions for the organisation and its mission and their own common sense when it comes to getting the most out of the people they have" (Vaill, 1989, pp. 19).

The role of emotional intelligence

Every way of leading has both advantages and disadvantages. For example, a leader can be remarkably kind and patient, yet lack assertiveness. On the other hand, another leader might handle conflict effectively, demonstrating impressive courage, but make enemies easily, and be ineffective at compromising when necessary. The best approach then, is to be an authentic leader with self-awareness. According to Evans (pp. 200), by taking this approach, one is better equipped to compensate for any limitations and is unlikely to dwell on them. Finally, the leader must not just advocate, but serve as an example of the changes desired before asking staff to do so.

This requires emotional intelligence, which according to Karen Ardley (2017) "is the ability to understand, use and manage our own emotions and respond to the emotions of others, in constructive and purposeful ways." The importance of emotional intelligence as a factor for creating better leaders is fundamental, since we cannot show leadership for others when we are not living it in our own lives.

In terms of self-awareness and management, we need to ensure that we manage our emotions in order to control our behaviours. The first step to developing positive leadership behaviours is to control our self-talk. Optimism, it would seem, is a key characteristic of the best leaders (just as it is a key characteristic of the best teachers). Numerous studies support this assertion, along with other benefits such as better health and increased longevity. The Nun Study (2003), originally led by Dr Snowden, is a particularly interesting example. The study shows that nuns who expressed more positive emotions lived, on average, a decade longer than their less optimistic peers and they were far less likely to develop Alzheimer's disease.

On the subject of emotional intelligence and leadership, Benjamin Zander's work serves as a useful analogy. Using the orchestra as a metaphor for leadership, one of my main takeaways from Benjamin Zander's TED talk in 2008 (The transformative power of classical music) is the idea that the conductor never makes a sound. In other words, the best leaders inspire leadership in others – and we can see it's working for our audience because of their "shining eyes". As Benjamin Zander explains, 'The eyes never lie. If the eyes are shining, then I know that my leadership is working.'

As a conductor of an orchestra, I realised the music was beautiful and I wasn't making a sound.

The conductor who does not make a sound can focus on making others more powerful. This makes sense: if the people you are managing feel connected, they are more likely to perform at their best. The same of course is true of teaching students.

The importance of high performing teams

The best schools are made up of teams that work well together. The quote by the British researcher and management theorist, Meredith Belbin, makes a pertinent point here:

Nobody's perfect but a team can be.

According to Karen Ardley, a high performing team:

– achieves high levels of leadership confidence

– build its capacity to implement change effectively

– nurtures energy and enthusiasm for learning and teaching

– develops and shares its knowledge, skills and expertise

– builds esteem of all members

In order to better understand how to develop a team and get to the high-performing stage faster, Tuckman's 4 stage model (1965) for team development is a useful model:

At the **forming stage**, the leader needs to be directive – providing structure for the team and clarifying expectations about how the team process will be initiated.

During the **storming stage**, the leader coaches the group by helping them focus on the goals and expectations, managing process and conflict, generating ideas, and explaining decisions.

As the team enters the **norming stage**, the leader acts primarily as a facilitator by providing encouragement, helping to build consensus, and giving feedback.

Finally, at the **performing stage**, the leader still facilitates the team process, but tasks and objectives are delegated. The leader oversees and identifies when the group is moving to a different stage.

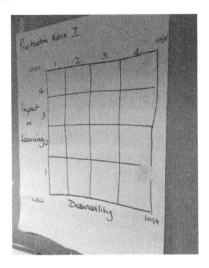

New initiatives for teaching and learning are rolled out on a regular basis. In terms of assessing the level of priority that should be given to these different initiatives, Karen Prioritisation Matrix can be useful. In this example, the team agreed that Assessment for Learning (AfL) is of high desirability and has a high impact on learning – it should therefore be given top priority as an initiative in the school setting.

Practising leadership

Meetings

As obvious (or not) as it may sound, the best meetings are fun and enjoyable. Essentially, they are conversations that lead to action – they are not about information giving. This requires a clear and purposeful agenda (timed, prioritised), ground rules (listen with an open mind, encourage everyone to participate) and the use of relevant materials (post-its, pens, paper, etc.)

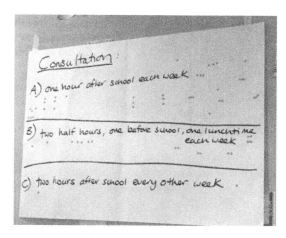

For larger teams, the method shown in the image above, of using dot stickers can serve to quickly gauge and visually represent the popularity of the team's preference when there are two or more possible options over an issue. In this hypothetical example, the team has been asked about our preference regarding when to hold a team meeting. They needed to use three stickers for their strongest preference, two stickers for their second-best choice and one (or no stickers) for their least desired choice.

Challenging people

For difficult conversations, which you will almost certainly have at some point, you should do the following:

- Choose the location

- Plan and script

- Predict likely responses

- Use assertive statements

- Think win:win

It is also worth explaining how you are made to feel by the other person's behaviour, since nobody can deny your feelings.

Shaping school culture & promoting core values

Shaping school culture begins with effective leadership, which then permeates and fosters positive change throughout the school. This is because effective leadership influences everyone who works for a school, and each one of these staff members is either directly or indirectly responsible for students' learning. For a school leadership and culture to be successful therefore, it needs everyone on board, facilitating educational experiences that cater for students' interests, innate desire for creativity, and a need for play. Teaching staff, administration and support personnel must work collaboratively in order to create a learning experience that will bring significant value to students.

According to Eric Sheninger, author of Uncommon Learning, there are several key ingredients to effective leadership that promote a positive school culture:

1. **Clear vision and communication** – According to Leithwood & Riehl (*What we know about successful school leadership,* 2003), effective leaders help their schools develop or endorse visions that embody the best thinking about teaching and learning while inspiring others to reach for ambitious goals. In the digital world, leaders can use a variety of communication channels to reach all possible stakeholders. In addition to memos, meetings, newsletters, and email, messages can be amplified using social media tools such as Google Classroom, Twitter, Facebook, and Instagram.

2. **Allowing for autonomy and ownership** – Unprecedented learning opportunities can take place when school leadership gives up some control, allowing learners (teachers included!) to explore their own passions and interests, enabling them to take ownership of their learning, while helping the community to develop growth mindsets. According to Blackwell, Trzesniewski, & Dweck (2007), learners with growth mindsets have been found to be more motivated to learn and exert effort and outperform those with fixed mindsets. An excellent example of autonomy and ownership in classroom practice is Genius Hour (see Chapter 28 for more information). Motivated by curiosity and passion, the big idea for Google was that employees would be happier, more creative, and more productive, which benefitted the company in terms of morale and overall performance. This concept can be transferred to the school system by allowing teachers and students time to explore their own curiosity, and then integrating this time into opportunities for meaningful teaching and learning.

3. **Collaboration** – Empowering teachers to work and collaborate toward a common goal makes them aware of their responsibilities and the important role each one of them plays in the work (Hughes & Pickeral, 2013). Again, this requires allocating time specifically for this purpose. Well planned collaborative workshops can be a great way for teachers to share ideas about professional practice.

4. **Modelling** – Initiating sustainable change requires educators to model the same expectations that they have of others. This is true of teachers and

leaders alike. Setting a direction and helping people implement a change are imperative for the successful implementation of any initiative. Eric Sheninger (2016) makes a very valuable point in his book 'Uncommon Learning', that we should move away from telling people what to do, and instead take them where they need to be. According to Sheninger, 'if you want change, model it. Modelling the way is one of the best things a leader can do to move others down a different path to initiate and sustain change.'

5. **Promote Risk Taking** – The right culture encourages teachers to try new strategies and activities in the classroom. In such an environment, teachers feel they have the autonomy and support to be as innovative as they want. The same is true for students. As Branden (1994) states in 'The Six Pillars of Self-Esteem', students who feel empowered are more confident and exhibit more self-esteem. Confidence can increase a person's ability to think and cope with basic challenges. Self-esteem can increase feeling worthy and the ability to assert one's needs and wants.

6. **Support** – Time, professional learning, infrastructure, and resources are all areas of support that help to create a positive school culture. Teachers need time for example, to innovate, try new things, and learn. In particular, schools need to consider ways to free up teachers from meaningless meetings and instead use that time for professional development. My own experience of this is through the delivery of workshops, which I always strive to make as fun and engaging as possible. After all, what we feel we remember, which is why attaching emotion to learning is so impactful! As professional development time with teachers can be short (usually, a training workshop lasts just one hour), I believe there are three key elements to making workshops for teachers successful:

– the core idea must be presented as simply as possible

– the training must allow for creative expression

– at least one new skill must have been acquired by the end of the session

In other words, fun & engaging PD workshops = easy to grasp + allows for creative expression + provides new skill(s)

Shared vision, effective communication, autonomy, collaboration, modelling, risk taking and support all contribute to a transformational school culture, which leads to greater levels of teacher satisfaction and student achievement.

Core values are what support the vision, shape the culture and reflect what the school values. They are the essence of the school's identity by reflecting the community's beliefs about what it considers to be the most important desirable qualities to guide everybody's behaviour. As with any organisation, schools with a culture of strong core values are likely to do better than those without a strong core value system. By "strong" I mean to say that the values should be alive within the school culture – exemplified through the activities, attitudes and behaviours of all key members of the school community, including school leadership, teachers and students.

School must create a "values-based" culture if they are to be successful at nurturing a happy community of students (and staff) who will make the most of their teaching & learning opportunities. An interesting point made by Ron Berger, author of An Ethic of Excellence (2003, pp. 41), is that the power of the culture rests in community:

When I've visited effective schools, I've been struck with the realisation that though the settings and resources are often widely different, every school I've seen has a strong sense of community… Students and staff in all these settings feel they are part of something – they belong to something.

I provide several examples here from my experiences in previous schools of ways in which such core values can be brought to life within any school setting.

Compassion

In my previous school in El Salvador, we used the student council as a vehicle to promote school values. This senior student pictured here were just one of a dozen senior students who were instructed to read fables to children in lower primary and then discuss the moral message afterwards.

Another project we initiated in El Salvador was a mentoring programme, which paired 8 senior students with younger peers in primary to mentor for a couple of hours each week. The programme lasted for a full academic year. By serving as positive role models, this was a rewarding experience for both mentors and mentees.

In order to tackle behavioural problems that were taking place in the school playground, the school council was also directed to design various floor-based games, including twister and hopscotch. In addition to purchasing a range of new playground toys such as skipping ropes, hula-hoops and balls, we ran a school council assembly to introduce the revamped school playground and outline behavior expectations during break times.

The floor-based games, such as hopscotch and four squares, which were painted on our school playground, provided many opportunities for us to share and reinforce our vision of caring children, who look after one another. For example, it gave us an opportunity to look closely at the rules of the games with the children and this in turn promoted discussion about what it means to be 'caring'.

Determination

By providing challenging activities, which require creative problem solving on the part of students, determination is certainly a value that can be nurtured. The students pictured above were involved in a whole school science fair in which different groups of students were competing against one another to showcase their science experiments. On the final day, the senior leadership team went around the school as judges to evaluate the projects and present awards.

Related to this idea, an important point made by Ron Berger is that it is through students' own work that their self-esteem will grow:

When they can begin to make discoveries that impress their classmates, solve problems as part of a group, put together projects that are admired by others, produce work of real quality, a new self-image as a proud student will emerge.

Integrity

In my early days of teaching in London, I organised a Young Enterprise initiative for students. Drawing on a pool of willing secondary school students to help facilitate the programme, this effectively gave all students involved a real-world project in which to learn financial literacy through business education. Real world projects, I believe, are a great way to teach values such as integrity. By giving students an idea about how their actions can impact others in a real-world context (global trade in this example), they can begin to see the application of values such as integrity to their daily lives.

Pupils are discovering business and economics thanks to innovative teaching events.

Flair trade

They are days to discover commerce and trade rather than geography or English.

At Barham Primary School, Year 6 took part in a Young Enterprise Day recently to help teach pupils more about economics and business. The school teamed up with the enterprise education charity, Young Enterprise, and Wembley High Technology College to organise the day, which used games and activities to teach the subjects.

from Wembley High School who volunteered to help run the special event and had received special training from staff at Young Enterprise. It followed core teaching about economics and business in the National Curriculum.

"It was a great session in which the students worked well together in teams to utilise their

At Kingsbury High School around 160 students from Year 9 and Year 10 took part in a day, simulating real-life trading, using maths, enterprise and team-building skills.

The fast-paced students traded oil, reacted to market news and managed budgets in six trading rounds, which tested their teamwork and understanding of economics.

The trade gave students the opportunity to see how maths and mathematical models

Finally, it is important that values are visible for the school community. Again, this can be a great project for the School Council to take on – creating displays of the school's values for everyone in the community to see.

Enlisting the help of our Art teacher, we had the School Council paint the school's values on the playground walls. It was not long before everyone in the community knew what the school values were because they saw them every day!

Every classroom also had the school values displayed on one of the walls in both English and their native language, Spanish.

Our school's shared vision, *'A caring community, striving for excellence, where every individual matters'*, was well embedded in everything we had been doing. For PSHE lessons for example, we emphasised the need to be a 'caring' individual, and we reinforced this with the children (and their parents) whenever conflicts arose. Our School Council was also used as a vehicle to support this vision, leading to various fundraising initiatives.

Many of our teachers received training on the concept of growth mindset, so they knew how important it was that we were all seen to be 'striving for excellence'. As well as modelling this principle for our children by teaching to a high standard, we would use our learner profile certificate system and house points, to recognise and reward effort. As all schools should do, we displayed and celebrated children's work throughout the school, both in classrooms and corridors. Our children were thus motivated to continually strive to do their best.

Whatever the school context, from my experience, the whole community plays a critical role in bringing school values alive. By embedding the school values into teaching and learning opportunities, bringing different

114

sections of the school to work together and ensuring the values are made explicit through displays, a values-based culture can be created. This can take a lot of time and energy to implement, but the benefits will be felt throughout the wider community for a long time to come.

15. School Trips & Team Building

School trips offer a fantastic opportunity for providing students with a completely new learning environment to what they are used to. I can still remember, at 9 years old, going on my first school residential trip to the Lake District in England. Being outdoors in nature was both exhilarating and rejuvenating. It was so much fun: abseiling, hiking, orienteering, sleeping in dorms, buying glow worms – not to mention playing in a huge adventure park! As I have already mentioned at the beginning of this book, I was far from academic in those early days, but that did not matter in the slightest. On the contrary, being outdoors in a completely different setting offered me a different type of education. It gave me the opportunity to learn about the natural environment, to build new social relationships and to develop interpersonally. I would even go so far as to say, that my fondest memories of school at that time, were from those five-days that I spent in the Lake District. In all the school trips that I have led since both as a teacher and a school leader, I know that for most young people, the opportunity to go on a residential trip can one of the most wonderful and memorable experiences that they will have at school – especially in this day and age.

Child-advocacy expert, Richard Louv (2008), makes a compelling case for the importance of nature in children's lives. Louv refers to the current generation of children as 'nature-deficit', to describe the human costs of alienation from nature. These costs, according to Louv, include some of the most disturbing childhood trends, such as rises in obesity, Attention Deficit Disorder (ADD) and depression.

Nature inspires creativity in a child by demanding visualization and full use of the senses. Given a chance, a child will bring the confusion of the world to the woods, wash it in the creek, turn it over to see what lives on the unseen side of that confusion. Nature can frighten a child, too, and this fright serves a purpose. In nature, a child finds freedom, fantasy, and privacy: a place distant from the adult world, a separate place (Louv, 2008, pp. 7).

I think we all intuitively know about the necessity of contact with nature for healthy child – and adult – development. Indeed, a growing body of research links our mental, physical, and spiritual health directly to our association with nature – in positive ways (Louv, 2008, pp. 3). Similarly, according to Sigurd Olsen (1967), renowned wilderness writer, the need for risk, adventure and self-sufficiency are sought after because they are basic human needs that the outdoors provides.

From the standpoint of successful teaching, it is important to seek out opportunities for helping to organise and lead school trips, especially those, which give young people the opportunity to be outdoors in nature. Using the outdoor environment not only facilitates diverse learning opportunities, it gives you the opportunity to build a stronger rapport with the students, one based on values such as collaboration, international-mindedness and respect.

Planning and leading a school trip has much in common with planning and leading a military operation. You do a reconnaissance (known in teaching terms as a 'pre-visit'), complete a thorough risk assessment, discuss the trip with your senior leaders, go over the plans with your colleagues and then get everything ready to mobilise your troops (the children). Having been involved with and led many school residential trips, I would say the key to making them a success is organisation.

After all the bookings have been done (accommodation, buses, excursions, school iPads, etc.), permission slips and medical forms have been collected, and groups have been organised, it is necessary to make sure that everyone has a clear idea of what they should be doing. For this, I provide each teacher with their own colour-coded folder, which contains everything they must know, including: staff expectations, bus groupings, room lists, maps, timetables and information about activities. You can view exemplars of the information and activities shared with staff and students in the appendix.

116

Team building games

Team building games can be an effective way to teach young people about the importance of group cohesion and values. As tools for human connection, they can be just as useful for the school context as they are for residential trips. They can also be great to use at the beginning of the school year, as an icebreaker, to help get to know your students better. For maximum impact, team building games should end with a debrief, to consolidate everyone's understanding of the lesson behind the game. Before moving onto Part Three of this book, I list some examples here of my favourite team building games to use with students, which require minimal resources.

1. **Human knot**
   Students are to be instructed to form a circle. Whilst in the circle they should stretch out their arms, to hold hands with someone else in the circle (but not both hands the same person). The challenge is then for the students to untie the knot without letting go of their hands.
   Discussion points: communication, determination and teamwork.

2. **Minefield**
   Create an area full of obstacles. The task will be for students to cross that area one at a time, blindfolded, without touching any obstacles. In order to be able to cross the minefield successfully, they need to be guided by the others who are outside of the minefield area.
   Discussion points: communication, listening and strategy.

3. **Lava River**
   Divide the group into two and point to an area on the ground where the "lava river" is, making sure everyone knows this cannot be touched. Each group will start on either side of the lava river with the task being to get to the other side. The only way to get to the other side is by using a limited number of lava proof mats, which the students have to work out how to use. If one of the students accidentally touches the lava river, they lose one of their mats and have to start again at the beginning.
   Discussion points: teamwork and strategy.

4. **Who stole my water bottle?**
   Stand facing away from the students with the water bottle behind you. The whole group should be relatively far behind you (behind a line), facing your back and are only allowed to move while you are saying the phrase "who stole my water bottle?" By the end of this phrase, you should turn around and all the students should be frozen like statues. Students win if they can bring the bottle and

the group back to their starting line before you turn around. It is a lot easier if they pass the bottle to other members of the group rather than trying to run alone.

Discussion points: teamwork, listening and strategy.

5. **Find the Tree**

In this activity, the whole group must cross a certain area together with their arms hooked. This is easy at first, so for the second attempt most of the group must do this blindfolded. The idea is to check if the blindfolded students will listen to the few students who can see, and follow their instructions.

Discussion points: Communication, listening and respect for when someone is talking.

16. Key Points from Part Two

- Students' learning automatically benefits when they feel a human connection with the key people around them – family, peers and of course, teachers.

- A key part of the work that we do as educators, is to teach children positive values. As principles that guide our thinking and behaviour, values are critical.

- The whole community plays a critical role in bringing school values alive. By embedding the school values into teaching and learning opportunities, a values-based culture can be created.

- Core values are what support the vision, shape the culture and reflect what the school values. They are the essence of the school's identity by reflecting the community's beliefs about what it considers to be the most important desirable qualities to guide everybody's behaviour.

- Effective behaviour management is the single most important foundation for successful teaching, and it is perhaps the most overlooked.

- Your emotions and consequent nonverbal cues have significant implications for students' behaviour in the classroom.

- Strive to always be positive not only with your own internal dialogue, but also with the dialogue that you have with students.

- Create an intelligent system of appropriate praise and sanctions, which motivates children to behave well because it feels good to do so.

- The classroom should be a home away from home for students with predictable routines and structured activities.

- When students do cause problems in your lessons, it is imperative that you keep excellent records and keep parents in the loop.

- Any communication with parents must come across as unemotional and clearly state the facts about what exactly happened as well as any follow-up action taken.

- Neither successful teaching nor learning can take place if the teacher is not rooted to the present moment.

- When faced with difficult situations, mindfulness practice can help you to achieve a state of equanimity and present moment awareness, which improves your teaching.

- Educators must have a working knowledge of child protection and safeguarding.

- Teachers must receive specific feedback if they are to grow.

- Feedback for teachers should be presented positively, focusing on what went well before outlining strategies for improvement.

- Effective leadership influences everyone who works for a school.

- School trips and team building activities offer effective opportunities to teach students values.

PART THREE

Teaching Strategies

The greatest sign of success for a teacher… is to be able to say, 'The children are now working as if I did not exist.'

- *Maria Montessori*

17. Applying Bloom's Taxonomy

It is fitting for the first chapter of this section on Teaching Strategies to be about Bloom's taxonomy[6]. As a framework to support teaching and learning, Bloom's taxonomy is the most widely used and enduring tool through which to think about students' learning. Originally created by the American educational psychologist, Benjamin Bloom in 1956, Bloom's taxonomy provides a hierarchical ordering of cognitive skills and is used worldwide to help inform successful teaching practice.

The creation of Bloom's taxonomy after the Second World War reflects the increasing importance of formal education to industrialised society. In a world in which formal education began to play a greater role than ever before, Bloom's taxonomy quickly became popular as a way to formalise teaching and learning practices, help write exams and develop curricula.

The fact that Bloom's taxonomy can be applied to any content intended for students to learn, is what makes this framework so powerful. It can be seen, to a greater or lesser extent, in all mark schemes and assessment objectives provided by all examining bodies in almost any curriculum subject. For teachers, Bloom's taxonomy is a practical tool to use, providing a framework in which to plan challenging lessons that help to ensure students' progress is maximised – a fundamental tenet of successful teaching. Among its many uses, Bloom's taxonomy provides an excellent foundation for lessons, as it can be used as a framework in which to deliver appropriate activities, assessment, questioning, objectives and outcomes.

It is worth taking the time therefore, to become familiar with the categories of the taxonomy, their order and their meaning. I illustrate Bloom's taxonomy[7] here, including some examples of keywords associated with each

---

[6] Bloom developed three taxonomies – each one for a different domain. This book refers only to the cognitive domain, which is used for classroom-based sessions. Skill-based sessions on the other hand, should employ the psychomotor domain, and group activities should employ the affective domain.
[7] The original Bloom's taxonomy for the cognitive domain was revised in 2001 Lorin Anderson and David Krathwohl. Among several changes made, the revision uses verbs (Remembering,

level (shown in *italics*).

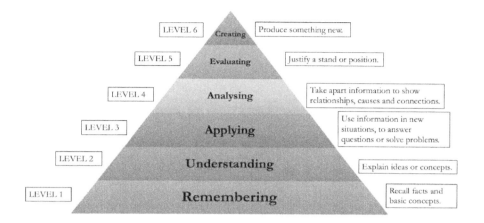

Level 1, **Remembering**, is the most basic, requiring the least amount of cognitive rigour. This is about students recalling key information, for example, the meaning of a word.

Arrange	*Define*	*Describe*	*List*	*Match*	*Name*	*Order*	*Recall*	*Reproduce*

Level 2, **Understanding**, is to do with students demonstrating an understanding of the facts remembered. At this level, the student who recalls the definition of a word, for example, would also be able to show understanding of the word by using it in the context of different sentences.

Classify	*Discuss*	*Explain*	*Identify*	*Report*	*Summarise*

Level 3, **Applying**, is concerned with how students can take their

---

Understanding, etc.) instead of nouns, providing learners with clearer objectives for what is expected of them. 'Synthesis' was replaced with 'Creating', and the new version also swaps the final two levels, Synthesis/Evaluation, making 'Creating' the ultimate level achievable. Lorin Anderson and David Krathwohl were well placed to make these revisions; Lorin Anderson was Benjamin Bloom's former student, and David Krathwohl was one of Bloom's partners who helped to devise the classic cognitive taxonomy. I refer here only to the new version.

knowledge and understanding, applying it to different situations. This usually involves students answering questions or solving problems.

Apply	Calculate	Demonstrate	Interpret	Show	Solve	Suggest

Level 4, **Analysing**, is about students being able to draw connections between ideas, thinking critically, to break down information into the sum of its parts.

Analyse	Appraise	Compare	Contrast	Distinguish	Explore	Infer	Investigate

Level 5, **Evaluating**, is reached when students can make accurate assessments or judgements about different concepts. Students can make inferences, find effective solutions to problems and justify conclusions, while drawing on their knowledge and understanding.

Argue	Assess	Critique	Defend	Evaluate	Judge	Justify

Level 6, **Creating**, is the ultimate aim of students' learning journey. At this final level of Bloom's taxonomy, students demonstrate what they have learnt by creating something new, either tangible or conceptual. This might include, for example, writing a report, creating a computer program, or revising a process to improve its results.

Compose	Construct	Create	Devise	Generate	Organise	Plan	Produce

As Bloom's taxonomy is a hierarchy of progressive processes ranging from the simple to the complex, in which it is necessary to first master those lower down the pyramid before being able to master those higher up, the framework promotes what Bloom termed 'mastery learning'. (We explore mastery learning as an evidence-based teaching strategy in Chapter 22.) The notion implies that almost all students have the potential to master any subject of knowledge simply by having enough time to do so and by being guided to move up through the taxonomy. This is because at each higher level of the taxonomy, students become more knowledgeable, more skilled and develop an improved understanding of the content they are learning. Thus, by creating lesson plans and tasks, using the examples of verbs (in italics) provided, teachers can align with the different levels of the taxonomy.

By simply moving to the higher levels of Bloom's taxonomy, these verbs can serve as the basis for learning objectives, questions or activities. They describe what we want students to be able to do, cognitively, with the content about which the students are learning. The higher up the pyramid of course, the more complex are the cognitive processes involved and, as such, ask students to engage in more challenging cognitive work connected to their lesson's content. As part of successful teaching practice, it can be necessary to scale back challenge in accordance with the response it draws, moving down the taxonomy as necessary.

A lesson could be planned about the benefits of renewable resources, the Roman empire, building a website or one of Shakespeare's sonnets. In all these examples, Bloom's taxonomy can be applied. An important point to consider, however, is that there can be occasions, particularly when first introducing a topic, where it is necessary to spend longer on the lower levels of the taxonomy. On such occasions, we do not seek to scale multiple levels of the taxonomy in a single lesson, instead choosing to do this over the course of a few lessons, due to the nature of the content (Gershon, 2015, pp. 103).

For example, for a series of Computing lessons that teach students how to build a webpage, the first lesson could explain to them about HTML, leading to a discussion about an example of HTML script and how it translates into a webpage (Level 1 – Remembering), before asking them to explain the purpose of different parts of the HTML script (Level 2 – Understanding). Students would move on to applying their knowledge and understanding of HTML, to begin building their own basic webpage, requiring them to solve any problems in their script (Level 3 – Applying), and then investigating additional features that could be added to their webpage (Level 4 – Analysing). As the lessons continue, students could be challenged further to critique their website, assessing its strengths and how it could be improved (Level 5 – Understanding). At the pinnacle of Bloom's taxonomy, it would be expected for students to create something completely new or original, producing a website that fulfils a particular purpose (Level 6 – Creating).

Similarly, for a series of literacy lessons looking at John Yeats' poem, 'The Lake Isle of Innisfree', the following tasks could be set according to each category of Bloom's taxonomy. After reading the poem together as a class, students could be asked to recite the first stanza of this poem (Level 1 – Remembering), before being asked where Yeats would like to be, London or the Lake Isle of Innisfree (Level 2 – Understanding). Afterwards, students could move on by describing the structure of Yeats' poem, explaining his use of rhythm and rhyme (Level 3 – Applying). In the subsequent lesson, students might be asked to analyse the mood of this poem, exploring how mood is created (Level 4 – Analysing). Later on, students could be asked to pick one of the images from the poem, evaluating its effectiveness (Level 5 – Evaluating). Finally, an appropriate activity to this finish off the topic might be to get the students to write their own poem on a similar theme (Level 6 – Creating).

Another point to make clear is that the separate processes of the taxonomy can be adapted according to the age-group and ability of students, enabling them to access the different levels of taxonomy according to the overall depth of their cognition. Level 6, Creating, for example, is obviously not going to be the same for a five-year old as it would be for a sixteen-year old. Nevertheless, the hierarchy of the different levels of the taxonomy remains the same.

In this way, Bloom's taxonomy is related to Bruner's notion of the spiral curriculum. This idea posits that students should return to key concepts and ideas at different points on their learning journey, each time meeting them at a more advanced stage of development. At whatever depth of cognition students access their lesson's content then, Bloom's taxonomy can help teachers to ensure that students are challenged.

18. Activities & Questioning

Before moving onto the many nuances that make up evidence-based teaching, it is important that we explore the topic of activities and questioning – the fundamental tools all teachers use daily. Both activities and questioning require students to use different cognitive processes to interact with lesson content. The quality of activities set and questions asked has a direct impact on the progress that students make. By aligning these with Bloom's taxonomy, cognitive demands are made on students, which can facilitate more challenge and help ensure rapid learning.

In the tables that follow, I provide exemplar question stems and sample activities for each level of Bloom's taxonomy. Having made several minor changes, I have assembled these tables using ideas from Dalton & Smith (1986), adapting their work according to the revised taxonomy. Although these lists are not exhaustive, they do provide an excellent starting point for how to use Bloom's taxonomy in the classroom.

Remembering	
Example Questions	**Sample Activities**
What happened after...? How many...? Who was it that...? Can you name the...? Describe what happened at...? Who spoke to...? Can you tell why...? Find the meaning of...? What is...? Which is true or false...?	Make a list of the main events. Make a timeline of events. Make a facts chart. Write a list of any pieces of information you can remember. List all the .... in the story/article/reading piece. Make a chart showing...

Understanding	
Example Questions	**Sample Activities**
Can you write in your own words...? Can you write a brief outline...? What do you think could have happened next...? Who do you think...? What was the main idea...? Who was the key character...? Can you distinguish between...? What differences exist between...? Can you provide an example of what you mean...? Can you provide a definition for...?	Illustrate what you think the main idea was. Make a cartoon strip showing the sequence of events. Write and perform a play based on the story. Retell the story in your words. Paint a picture of some aspect you like. Write a summary report of an event. Prepare a flow chart to illustrate the sequence of events.

Applying	
Example Questions	**Sample Activities**

Do you know another instance where...?	Construct a model to demonstrate how it will work.
Could this have happened in...?	Make a scrapbook about the areas of study.
Can you group by characteristics such as...?	Take a collection of photographs to demonstrate a particular point.
What factors would you change if...?	Make a clay model of an item in the material.
Can you apply the method used to some experience of your own...?	Design a market strategy for your product using a known strategy.

Analysing	
Example Questions	**Sample Activities**
Which events could have happened...?	Design a questionnaire to gather information.
How was this similar to...?	Write a commercial to sell a new product.
What was the underlying theme of...?	Conduct an investigation to produce information to support a view.
What do you see as other possible outcomes?	Make a flow chart to show the critical stages.
Why did ... changes occur?	Construct a graph to illustrate selected information.
Can you compare your ... with that presented in...?	Make a family tree showing relationships.
Can you explain what must have happened when...?	Prepare a report about the area of study.
How is ... similar to ...?	
What are some of the problems of...?	
Can you distinguish between...?	
What were some of the motives behind...?	
What was the problem with...?	

Evaluating	
Example Questions	**Sample Activities**
Is there a better solution to...?	Conduct a debate about an issue of special interest.
Judge the value of...	Make a booklet about 5 rules you see as important. Convince others.
Can you defend your position about...?	Form a panel to discuss views, e.g. "Learning at School.".
Do you think ... is a good or a bad thing?	

How would you have handled...? What changes to ... would you recommend? Do you believe...? Are you a ... person? How would you feel if...? How effective are...? What do you think about...?	Write a letter to ... advising on changes needed at... Write a report. Prepare a case to present your view about...

Creating	
Example Questions	**Sample Activities**
Can you see a possible solution to...? If you had access to all resources how would you deal with...? What would happen if...? Can you create new and unusual uses for...? Can you write a new recipe for a tasty dish? Can you develop a proposal which would...?	Invent a machine to do a specific task. Design a building to house your study. Create a new product. Give it a name and plan a marketing campaign. Write about your feelings in relation to... Write a TV show, play, puppet show, role play, song or pantomime about...? Design a record, book, or magazine cover for...? Sell an idea. Devise a way to... Compose a rhythm or put new words to a known melody.

As a final example, let's take a look at a stepped questioning activity, in which a series of questions are asked (written down or verbally) that gradually move up the levels of Bloom's taxonomy. Such an activity could be carried out during one single lesson:

1. What can you remember about the story? (Remembering)
2. Summarise the story in your own words. (Understanding)
3. Suggest how the main lessons in this story could help other young people. (Applying)

4. Why did the different characters in the story behave the way that they did? (Analysing)
5. Evaluate the strength of the main character's decision to leave. (Evaluating)
6. Rewrite the ending of this story, to show a different outcome. (Creating)

The framework is logical: each question becomes increasingly more challenging in terms of the cognitive demand placed on students. Stepped questions like these can be set as a single activity, with students working individually or in pairs. There is differentiation by outcome, as some students will get further than others, depending on their prior knowledge and understanding.

As all these examples highlight, Bloom's taxonomy provides a strong basis for tailored questioning and bespoke activities, in which we adapt and modify questions and activities in order to more closely meet the needs of the students. For instance, the teacher could start with a series of 'remembering' (knowledge) questions or activities before moving onto a set that focus on comprehension. It may well become apparent at this stage that the students are getting stuck at this level. The point is, depending on the answers elicited, the teacher can move up the taxonomy more quickly or more slowly until the appropriate level of challenge is reached. Having arrived at the appropriate level of challenge, successful teaching would pursue question stems and relevant activities such as those listed, to help push students' cognition, or to help them become unstuck in areas that were previously too challenging.

19. Evidence-Based Teaching

From a purely strategic perspective, there are three rules that must be followed if successful teaching is to happen. The teacher must:

1. Hold students' full attention;

2. Deliver memorable learning experiences;

3. Systematically check students' learning.

Every approach to teaching, educational policy, curriculum or pedagogical initiative is ultimately intended to meet one or more of these three rules.

As teaching is such a complex phenomenon, it helps to identify the most effective teaching strategies to help students learn – which meet these rules. To get us started, it is valuable to look at John Hattie's research. John

Hattie is a Professor of Education from New Zealand and a key proponent of **evidence-based teaching**. Evidence-based teaching is to teach using only those methods that have been verified from evidence to be effective. John Hattie is particularly notable for his work on what he terms 'Visible Learning', which is the world's largest ever collection of evidence-based research into what actually works in education. John Hattie headed a team of researchers for twenty years who trawled the world for evidence (taken from meta-studies) about the effectiveness of different teaching interventions. The good news from these studies is that 95% or more of things that teachers do to enhance the achievement of students in the classroom work. Taking this evidence though, which John Hattie presents as a continuum of achievement, his fundamental interest has been to pull out and share the **most effective** of these teaching interventions. For this reason, I greatly admire the work John Hattie and his team have done to further our understanding about what constitutes successful teaching.

When successful teaching is taking place, it stands to reason that learning is visible. This means that teachers know if learning is happening or not, and students know what to do and how to do it. The key idea of John Hattie's book, Visible Learning for Teachers, is that teachers and leaders should always be aware of the impact they are having on their students, and from the evidence of this impact, decisions must be made about changing approaches.

Using his data, John Hattie has identified the following qualities for teachers to have, which impact student learning the most (ordered here from 1 to 6 in order of importance):

1. Are **passionate** about helping their students learn

2. **Monitor** their impact on students' learning, and adjust their approaches accordingly

3. Are **clear** about what they want their students to learn

4. Forge strong **relationships** with their students

5. Adopt **evidence-based teaching** strategies (see Chapter 22)

6. Actively **seek to improve** their own teaching

Teachers are far more likely to have a low (or even negative) impact if they:

- Repeat students

- Label students (fixed mindset)

- Have low expectations

One of the major messages from Visible Learning is the power of teachers learning from and talking to each other about planning – learning intentions, success criteria, what is valuable learning, progression, what it means to be 'good at' a subject (Hattie, 2012, pp. 67). The key message here is clear – educators should not work in isolation. Hattie explains that schools must create the structures and cultures that foster effective educator collaboration – collaboration that focuses on their sphere of influence to impact student learning in a positive way.

That being said, before any teaching strategies are used, Hattie builds on Piaget's research (1970), to reassert the importance of teachers' understanding about how each student thinks. In other words, the teacher needs to understand where a student is in their level of thinking and then challenge each student accordingly to go beyond that level through a process described as 'cognitive acceleration'. Naturally, this should lead the teacher to differentiate activities during a lesson. Contrary to popular belief, differentiation is not a specific strategy but rather the application of a range of strategies. The specific strategies that follow are examples that can be used for differentiation.

20. The Power of Stories

When it comes to understanding how students think, cognitive psychology can help enormously. It has already been shown in Part Two for example, that just helping students to understand the meaning of a lesson goes a long way to help with their learning process. One of the key strategies that the cognitive scientist, Daniel Willingham (2009, pp.66-67) puts forward, for helping students to think about the meaning of a lesson, is to use stories:

'The human mind seems exquisitely tuned to understand and remember stories – so much so that psychologists sometimes refer to stories as "psychologically privileged", meaning that they are treated differently in memory than other types of material.'

Willingham identifies several important advantages of using a story structure when teaching, including the fact that:

1. Stories are easy to comprehend, because the audience knows the structure, which helps to interpret the action.

2. Stories are interesting.

3. Stories are easy to remember.

Stories of course, are just one way to get students to think about meaning.

Other approaches might include questioning, role-playing or well-crafted problem-solving activities. In situations where there is no meaning such as having to learn the spelling of odd words, then simple memory tricks like mnemonics are just as effective.

21. Pictorial Representation

Alongside stories, pictorial representation can be a powerful means to help learners remember new information and understand meaning. As a student and then again as a teacher, I would spend a great deal of time finding ways to present information visually. From drawing spider diagrams and mind maps, to colour coding text and using memorable images, I found these to be effective techniques for learning new concepts and ideas. Studies do indeed show that "a picture is worth a thousand words", and people tend to remember information better when it is presented in the form of pictures rather than words (e.g., Shepard, 1967). In part at least, this might be because pictures require a greater level of conceptual processing than words, potentially leading to better retention of pictorial representations (McBride & Dosher, 2002). It is well worth looking at ways then, of incorporating as much pictorial representation as possible into your teaching.

22. Feedback & Other High Impact Strategies

In Part Two, we looked at the importance of quality feedback for teachers to improve their teaching. We now turn to the quality of feedback given by teachers to their students. This is because, next to the method of instruction and lesson delivery, feedback is an incredibly powerful influence on student achievement. For feedback to be effective, Crooks (2001) states that the greatest motivational benefits will come from focusing feedback on:

- the qualities of the child's work, and not on comparison with other children,

- specific ways in which the child's work can be improved,

- improvements that the child has made compared to his or her earlier work.

According to Hattie & Clark (2019, pp. 136), the most valuable feedback is the 'in the moment' feedback, verbal or written, which teachers engage with throughout the lesson. Delayed feedback, for example in the form of teacher comments, can also be useful – so long as learners have the skill to interpret this feedback and that it helps to move the learners forward.

Butler's (1988) famous study in which students were given either: a) grades only, b) comment only or c) grades and comments found that those in the comment only groups had greater gains in progress (measured by test results) than the other two groups. In cases where positive comments accompanied grades, interviews with students revealed that they ignored those comments in favour of the grade and what it was telling them about their performance. As Hattie & Clark (2019) explain, grades often tell the students 'the work is over' and for this reason, we must not confuse grading with feedback. Although grades can be an indicator of student performance, effective feedback focuses on helping students to improve, providing 'where to next' or 'how to improve this work' information. Clark (2001) also notes that feedback must be easy to understand and time must be allocated for students to read the comments, to use them to improve.

Other high-impact, evidence-based teaching strategies that Hattie has identified include:

- *Note Taking & Other Study Skills* – by teaching not just content, but also study skills, students achieve deeper levels of understanding.

- *Direct Instruction* – the explicit teaching of a skill-set using lectures or demonstrations, e.g. the deliberate action of explicitly teaching the students the strategies for how to read. It should not be confused with didactic teacher-led talking from the front. Direct Instruction has 7 main steps:
  1. Teacher specifies learning outcomes/intentions
  2. Teacher knows and communicates success criteria
  3. Builds commitment and engagement in learning task (the hook)
  4. Lesson design: input, model, check for understanding
  5. Guided practice
  6. Closure
  7. Independent practice

- *Spaced Practice* – it is the frequency of different practice opportunities for students rather than spending "more" time on a task that makes the difference. Logically, for a simple task, only brief rest periods are needed for the learning to be assimilated by students. For more complex tasks, longer rest periods are needed in order for the learning to be assimilated.

- *Teaching Metacognitive Skills* (learning how to learn) – this requires teachers to establish a supportive environment where students can make mistakes, celebrate their progress and share their thinking. Teachers should encourage students to learn from mistakes by asking deliberate questions

132

and providing constructive feedback, to elicit misconceptions and get students to reflect on their learning process.

- *Teaching Problem Solving Strategies* – these are the tools students can use when there is no obvious solution to a problem. Every subject area has problem solving strategies that can be employed to help tackle specific tasks and ensure that learning takes place. When teaching children how to read for instance, there are strategies to unpick and articulate unfamiliar words. Likewise, answering comprehension questions or answering multi-step mathematical problems requires students to skim, scan and highlight parts of a text, making inferences where necessary – all of which are skills that should be taught.

- *Reciprocal Teaching* (involves students working in pairs to teach each other what they have just learnt) – the emphasis is on teachers enabling students to learn and use strategies such as summarizing, questioning, clarifying. In doing so, students learn to monitor their own learning and thinking.

- *Mastery Learning* - breaks subject matter and learning content into units with clearly specified objectives which are pursued until they are achieved. Learners must demonstrate mastery on a particular unit, e.g. by achieving at least 80% on an end of unit test, before moving on to new material. Any students who do not achieve mastery should be provided with extra support.

- *Concept Mapping* – this is the graphical representation of what is being learned and how it connects to other concepts. The process of creating a concept map involves students in higher-order thinking as they work to consolidate their ideas and to integrate them with other concepts. It also enables students to develop a product that can be assessed by teachers to check the depth of students' understanding and identify potential misconceptions.

- *Worked Examples* – this generally consists of a problem statement and the necessary steps for a solution. This minimises the cognitive load for students, enabling them to concentrate on the processes that lead to the correct answer rather than just providing an answer.

From Hattie's perspective, the teacher is literally the change agent in the classroom, which is why direct instruction features high on the list. It is also another reason why it is particularly important for students to have the success criteria explained. This is because it helps students to develop their metacognitive skills. Students who are taught the success criteria are more strategic in their choice of learning strategies, and thus more likely to enjoy the success that will lead to an upward spiral of learning – which is where mastery learning comes in.

Teaching strategies that had little or no impact included:

- Giving students control over their learning

- Problem-based teaching and learning

- Teaching test-taking

- Catering to learning styles

- Inquiry-based teaching and learning

As Hattie explains, the variability amongst teachers is dramatic in the education system. Some teachers who do certain things have powerful effects on students' achievement, but half of teachers are not doing those things, so they are not getting the above-average effects. Using evidence, however, can make a huge difference. By distilling the teaching and learning strategies into a continuum of effectiveness for student achievement, John Hattie's work brings us much closer to understanding what successful teaching looks like in practice.

What is interesting here is that when we dig beneath many of these qualities of successful teaching, it becomes obvious just how important it is for teachers to be emotionally involved in the teaching process. When teachers are emotionally involved, they naturally bring passion into lessons, forge strong relationships with students and actively seek to improve their own teaching – key qualities of successful teaching according to John Hattie's research.

Pedagogically speaking, a whole range of different methods can be used, from conventional direct instruction to highly student-centred instruction. Any strategy, which gets teachers into a positive emotional state will also help to ensure successful teaching. Of course, there can be many factors that influence a teacher's emotional state. Among the factors that can be particularly effective in this regard is working in a high performance, supportive team. One of the key strategies of such teams is that they have coaches. Coaches can serve as 'suppliers of candour, providing individual leaders with the objective feedback needed to nourish their growth' (Sherman & Frea, 2004). Thus, according to Hattie (pp. 71 – 72),

'coaching is specific to working towards student outcomes. It is not counselling for adults; it is not reflection; it is not self-awareness; it is not mentoring or working alongside. Coaching is deliberate actions to help the adults to get the results from the

students – often by helping teachers to interpret evidence about the effect of their actions, and providing them with choices to more effectively gain these effects. There are three elements: the coach; the coached; and the agreed explicit goals of the coaching.'

23. Using Effective Assessment Strategies

Assessment of students' learning is itself a key teaching strategy. Much has already been written by other authors on the subject of assessment. Nonetheless, for the purpose of this book, *Successful Teaching for Everyone*, it is necessary to define assessment, look at the best assessment strategies available to teachers and explain the evidence underlying these strategies. The problem, as noted by Fletcher-Wood (2018, pp. 25) is that many teachers use assessment techniques but have not really understood how such techniques are supposed to impact student learning. Often, teachers receive:

… a description of what to do and how to do it, but no description of why it might work. There is no explanation of the underlying learning principles on which the method or resources have been constructed. The result is that teachers are constantly being encouraged to try out new ideas or methods without understanding how they might be affecting student learning… Unless you have a good understanding of how the technique or resource is supposed to affect student learning, your adaptations can only be trial and error.' (Nuthall, 2007, pp. 14).

Let us start with the basics then. To put it simply, assessment is any method used to appraise the knowledge, skills or understanding that a student possesses. By providing feedback to students on their work, assessment is fundamental to the teaching and learning process because it can show teachers (and their students) what areas of students' performance needs to be improved. As Fletcher-Wood (2018, pp. 19) states:

Even if we thought we had created a perfect curriculum and predicted students' environments perfectly, we would still need assessment to check we were correct.

There are two types of assessment: summative assessment and formative assessment – referred to as assessment **of** learning and assessment **for** learning, respectively:

Summative assessments sum up what a student has achieved at the end of a period of time. Usually, a summative assessment is in the form of a test and is given at the end of a unit of work, at the end of a term, or at the end of a key stage. Whenever such an assessment is used, its purpose is to show the attainment of the student at a particular point in time and can be useful for tracking progress over time.

While summative assessment can be useful at providing a snapshot into the students' learning, for the purpose of cultivating successful teaching and substantially improving student achievement, evidence points to the huge value that can be made by formative assessment.

Formative assessments take place on an ongoing basis during teaching and learning, allowing both teachers and students to assess progress more frequently. A formative assessment may take the form of teacher questions, tasks, quizzes or even tests. Most frequently, formative assessments may not be recorded at all, except perhaps in the lesson plans designed to address the next steps indicated. Plenty of studies have demonstrated the substantial impact of formative assessment on student learning (Kingston and Nash, 2011). Ideally, to truly help students in the learning process, feedback from such formative assessments, must be given immediately and frequently.

It should be noted that the distinction provided here between these two main types of assessment (summative and formative) has to be treated quite loosely. This is because, in some situations, an assessment used summatively, for example an end of unit test, can also serve as a formative assessment. As Dylan Wiliam (2018, pp. 48) points out,

'An assessment functions formatively to the extent that evidence about student achievement is elicited, interpreted, and used by teachers, learners, or their peers to make decisions about the next steps in instruction that are likely to be better, or better founded, than the decisions they would have made in the absence of that evidence.'

What is widely referred to as 'responsive teaching' can also be seen as a key part of what is understood as successful teaching. As Fletcher-Wood (2018, pp. 22) describes it,

'Responsive teaching blends planning and teaching, based on an understanding of how students learn from cognitive science, with formative assessment to identify what students have learned and adapt accordingly.'

'Formative' in this context describes the function that the evidence serves, rather than the assessment itself. In other words, formative assessment involves getting the best possible evidence about what students have learned and then using this information to decide where to go next.

To accomplish this big idea, Wiliam provides five key strategies of formative assessment:

1. **Clarifying, sharing, and understanding learning intentions and success criteria**. After all, it is important that students know where they are going in their learning and what counts as quality

work. It is, however, up to teachers to exercise judgement in how best to communicate learning intentions and success criteria to students.

2. **Eliciting evidence of learning.** Once the teacher knows where learners are in their learning, he or she is in a position to carry out step 3.

3. **Providing feedback that moves learning forward.** Some ways to provide effective feedback have already been described following discussion of John Hattie's research. The key point here is that the feedback should cause a cognitive rather than an emotional reaction.

4. **Activating learners as instructional resources for one another.** Any technique that facilitates peer assessment, e.g. "think-pair-share" or peer marking, will force students to internalize the learning intentions and success criteria, which can be seen as stepping stones for step 5.

5. **Activating learners as owners of their own learning.** This takes time and the key here is to get students to reflect on their own learning. For example, many teachers use the traffic lights technique. At the beginning of the lesson, the teacher shares the learning intention and any associated success criteria, and then at the end of the lesson, students have to self-assess by placing a coloured circle next to the learning intention in their exercise books (e.g. green for confident, yellow for ambivalent and red for not confident). A variant of this strategy is simply getting the students to put their thumbs up if they feel confident and their thumbs down if they do not feel so confident with having met the learning intention. In this way, the teacher knows that it is necessary to return to, and possibly, adapt the teaching approach for those students who feel less confident with the teaching matter.

A similar strategy that I would use is a 'Stick it where it counts!' display. At the end of the lesson, I would ask learners to use the system of smiley faces pictured, to stick (using Velcro) the relevant face to where they felt they were in terms of their understanding of a particular lesson. I would then take a photo of this wall to use for my own records. At a glance, this strategy makes it is easy to see how well a lesson has gone and how much of the content needs to be revisited. Such approaches are often best combined with asking questions during the plenary, checking to see what students have learnt during the lesson and what their target is for the next lesson.

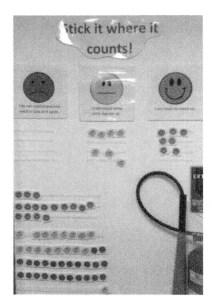

These techniques are just some ideas, which I have used as part of formative assessment. It should be noted that each teacher has to find out what works in his or her own context. The same techniques will work extremely well with some classes and cohorts but not with others. Teachers must 'adapt, adjust and make appropriate professional judgements' (Loughran, Berry and Mulhall, 2012, pp. 2).

Another approach, which I am a great proponent of, to activating learners as owners of their own learning is to use a system of digital portfolios. A portfolio is just a purposeful collection of student work, which can provide direct indicators of students' learning experiences over time. As Hardiman (2012, pp. 154-155) states, portfolios can be a powerful tool to demonstrate progress in attaining learning objectives, and such visible progress can be a strong motivator for students and teachers alike. In so doing, portfolio assessment encourage metacognition that permits students to set their own learning goals and then track their progress. Digital portfolios are particularly useful as well because they can serve as an administrative tool to manage and organise work created with different applications, which can then be shared on the web for the whole community to see.

As Woodward (2000) points out, the value of portfolios is thoroughly researched and their use in education is well documented. By demonstrating the development of knowledge, skills and understanding over time, digital portfolios make valuable assessment and learning tools. To ensure deep learning though, it is not enough for students to simply showcase a series of digital artefacts they have created. It is also important that students reflect on the work they have produced, and this can be done by simply getting them to write about what they have learnt. This helps to reinforce students' knowledge and understanding, which complement the skills they demonstrate through the creation of digital artefacts. In order to get students into the habit of developing decent digital portfolios, I would recommend that the process is started early – the last couple of years of primary school is a good time to start.

Project work lends itself particularly well to this process of building up a digital portfolio. A link to a game created in Scratch for example, with some commentary and reflection about the process of making the game, would provide evidence of a number of attainment targets. Over the course of the key stage, a diverse portfolio of evidence of student learning should emerge, which meets all the curriculum requirements. At any time, it also provides teachers with a snapshot of which attainment targets a student has met, and which still require more evidence. I would therefore suggest that a list of links to students' digital portfolios be placed on the same spreadsheet as that used for assessment of students' attainment. (These links can be collected easily using, for example, Survey Monkey or Google Forms).

In fact, recent advances in digital technology is making the administration and use of digital portfolios easier than ever. In the case of Ms Judith's lesson (Lesson Observation 1), the Seesaw app was used as the main medium in which to collect evidence of, showcase and provide feedback on students' work. Alternatively, Google Drive or Google Sites for example, can be just as effective – as I will explain.

In this video (https://youtu.be/YQRJSVY1C74) for instance, I show how you can use folders and subfolders within the Google Drive, so that students can upload their work, e.g. documents, photos and videos, into a digital student portfolio folder. The video then explains how such folders can be organised, shared with and made easily accessible for teachers using QR codes.

In order to motivate students and at the same time provide assessment for learning opportunities, digital badges could also be linked to the system of digital portfolios. A digital badge (embedded into the digital portfolio) is just a mini-credential, providing students with a validated indicator of accomplishment in a particular area. In this second video (https://www.youtube.com/watch?v=Y-SqQSyG3sw), you can see how Google Sites and digital badges can be integrated.

In the second example here, the idea is that students would earn digital badges according to the areas of learning they demonstrate across the statutory attainment targets (in this case, as set out from the UK Computing curriculum). It is important from the outset that though, that the badge information is shared with students in a straightforward language that can be easily understood. I would even say that the badge information itself should be embedded into the students' digital portfolios, so that students can clearly identify what knowledge, skills and understanding they need to demonstrate in order to earn a particular badge.

As this second video demonstrates, assessment of students' attainment feeds into the digital badge system quite easily, with badges for each of the attainment targets linked to relevant evidence on a student's digital portfolio.

If a school already has Google Apps for Education, which is free, it makes sense to make full use of this google ecosystem to integrate the assessment of students' attainment with digital portfolios. In this particular example, I was able to use Google Apps for Education to create an integrated assessment model in order to automatically issue digital badges to students upon having had their attainment graded by the teacher. It meant that students did not need another set of login information to access their digital badges and portfolios, and the school did not need to pay for premium services.

The main point is that whatever system is used for digital portfolios, students should keep this up-to-date to showcase and reflect on their learning. These digital portfolios then need to be easily accessible by teachers, so that accurate assessments of students' knowledge, skills and understanding is made possible. I would highly recommend such an assessment model, as it also frees up time for teachers to focus on properly appraising students' knowledge, skills and understanding across the curriculum. For students, the digital portfolio allows them to reflect on and keep track of what they have learnt, informing targets for what comes next. It gives parents a much more meaningful picture of what a child has learnt as well, and what they still need to study. Finally, it allows school leadership and the inspectorate to more accurately track year on year progress of students.

24. Case Study: Teaching Mathematics Successfully

Teaching mathematics successfully is a fundamental focus for policy in many countries, where the relationship between mathematical standards and the quality of the workforce, which maintains economic competitiveness, forms part of the government's rationale for wanting to improve numeracy standards. Recurring periods of national concern about low standards of numeracy skills shown by Primary school students have become more urgent and more political in recent years with the publication of international comparisons of mathematical achievement (Street et al., 2005, pp.1). In the UK, the National Curriculum offers a model for progression of learning in mathematics, and as with teaching across the developed world, this shows a focus in the way in which children learn as active problem solvers. Implicitly, this defines the ethos of constructivist' theories of how children learn and is based on the view that learners need to be actively engaged in constructing their own mathematical knowledge by seeking out meanings and making mental connections in an active manner.

Mathematics is both a body of established, recognised content and a process by which exploration and establishing takes place. As Brown (1989, pp. 126) states, there is mathematics to know and mathematics to do. Atkinson (1992, pp. 16) puts forward the view that the ability to solve problems is at the heart of mathematics. In the context of these widely accepted definitions of mathematics, progression in children's understanding of mathematics requires that in addition to having some knowledge of mathematical facts, concepts and skills, children are able to put their knowledge to work for the purpose of solving problems. Engaging in the processes of mathematical activity enables children to assimilate the associated skills and knowledge.

The role of the teacher can be viewed as crucial for enabling children to understand mathematics. As pointed out by Orton (1995, pp. 13), considerable emphasis in learning mathematics in recent times has been placed on the desirability of understanding rather than on being able to repeat remembered routines and demonstrate particular basic skills. Progression then, can be seen as the development of a child's ability and confidence to tackle the nature and purpose of mathematics whilst being able to explore and utilise a variety of mental strategies. There are many factors that facilitate progression, including the features of effective teaching and the extent to which students need to be accommodated.

For teachers to best support children's progression in their learning of mathematics, they must first plan lessons appropriately. Logically, this planning should be underpinned by an understanding of how children think and learn. As pointed out by Anghileri (1995, pp. 26), the new understandings which derive from all the current research into the processes by which children think and learn have clear and major implications for teaching mathematics to young children. Above everything else, the main implication is that it is the teacher's responsibility to nurture a positive attitude towards the subject of mathematics. In my own lessons that I taught, I certainly found that the students were much more engaged in learning when they enjoyed the activities that were associated with learning.

For example, I would make regular use of the interactive whiteboard for the purpose of virtual activities, which I found were effective in getting the children actively interested in the topic. Where possible, I made use of games that the children could play in pairs and groups. For one particular lesson on fractions, decimal & percentage equivalences, I got the children playing a game of dominoes in groups in which the object was to match the

142

correct equivalences. Interestingly, I tended to find that the use of games was not always conducive to forming a good basis for progression in children's understanding, since as much time would be spent on understanding the actual game as it would on gleaning understanding of the mathematics involved. They might well enjoy the activity of playing a game but the learning is often minimal. In addition, I would say that the effectiveness of any game or 'enjoyable activity' is largely determined by the extent to which it places mathematical problems in meaningful real-world contexts.

Indeed, making mathematics enjoyable should go hand in hand with making mathematics meaningful. This is the means by which anyone makes sense of anything new with which they are faced, by relating it to what is already known. As explained by Askew (1992, pp. 26) 'children working in Brazilian street markets demonstrated a range of mathematical skills and knowledge, which they had problems demonstrating in formal tests'. Arguably, activities used in classrooms need to mirror the sort of situations to which mathematics is actually applied. This must mean that this way of human learning is vastly inhibited when one is presented with information or experience that does not relate at all to what is known. Obviously, this has clear implications for the teaching of progression children's understanding of mathematics and leads a skillful teacher to place mathematics into a context in which the children are familiar.

Research, however, has shown that while practical work and 'real' contexts can be useful, they need to be chosen carefully, and accompanied careful dialogue with the students to establish the extent of their understanding (Askew, 1992, pp. 11). This has been confirmed by my own experience, as it is easy to spend too much time getting resources to fit a particular theme

143

or context but which can detract from the learning outcome. In order to get students really understanding mathematics, it is commonly agreed that students need to be supported in giving verbal explanations where they can talk through what they are doing, since this is an essential step in 'going mental'. Anghileri (1995, pp. 20) looks at the importance of children giving verbal explanations in terms of it being conducive to developing their cognitive awareness and control – that is, their ability to learn how to learn. This means children should be encouraged to be reflective about their own processing, and to adapt and develop strategies, which put them in control. In fact, this explains to a large extent the ethos behind the 'mental and oral starter'.

It is clear across all year groups that mathematical language used by the teacher regularly draws on 'open-targeted' questions, requiring the children to explain how they solved a problem. Insofar as helping children to learn strategies for understanding and applying mathematics, the mathematical language and mental strategies used is, according to Anghileri, important for enabling children to cope with what is known as structural limitation – that is, their limited memory capacity. This is achieved through children developing their selective attention, in which they sort out the relevant from the irrelevant, as well as developing their structural knowledge and processing strategies. In this way, they learn to chunk information together and improve the efficiency with which they assimilate new information.

The guidance given, as defined in the National Numeracy Strategy Framework in the UK, recommends that teachers should use effective questioning which allow children 'thinking' time, encourage explanation of methods and reasoning, and probe reasons for incorrect answers'. Many

144

studies have shown that the style of questioning is related to students' performance (Dillon,1985, pp.112). According to Dillon, the average differences in achievement of those classes whose teachers used demanding questions were, in some cases, equivalent to as much as one year's learning. Another significant aspect of a teacher's questioning style is the time that the teacher pauses after asking a question, before either supplying it themselves, or moving onto a different student (Tokin, 1986, pp. 198).

In terms of progression, I have found that in the lower year groups teachers mainly make use of closed and closed targeted questions, as there is less of an emphasis on the method of working but in the upper year groups more use is made of open and open-targeted questions. This makes sense because as children progress in their understanding of mathematics there becomes less of a need to recite patterns and more of a need to understand the actual working. Likewise, questioning is differentiated according to ability across a class as well as across year groups such that more open-ended style questioning in addition to the usual extension activities tends to be asked of the more able learners, particularly those who are 'gifted and talented'. My own observations have also revealed that simple statements made by the teacher help children to develop mental images, which in turn help them answer questions, e.g. 'put that number in your head because that is the first number we are counting…' Dillon (1985, pp. 114) suggests that when teachers make statements in order to provoke discussion rather than just ask questions, students can display more complex thought, deeper involvement, wider participation, greater interconnectedness, and richer inquiry.

It is in the application of this sort of teaching that common misconceptions can be addressed, exposed and discussed. From my own lesson observations and in fact my own teaching, I observed many misconceptions being demonstrated by students during the course of a lesson. It seems therefore, that to teach in a way that avoids creating any misconceptions is not possible, and that many of these misconceptions will remain hidden unless the teacher makes specific efforts to uncover them. A teacher's response to dealing with a child's mathematical error demands skill in diagnostic terms: different responses will be required depending on the nature and frequency of the error observed. For example, in one particular Year 6 lesson I was teaching, I remember there were several students who were over-generalising a pattern that is true for whole numbers but not true for decimal numbers such as in the case of $0.12 < 0.117$. Skill is needed on the part of the teacher to correctly ascertain why the children are making such mistakes so that they can be appropriately resolved. In the case of this particular lesson on Number, I could see the reason the children were making this mistake and was able to aid them in their understanding by speaking of 0.12 as 'one tenth, two hundredths' and 0.117 as 'one tenth one hundredth & seven thousandths'. The language used therefore, clearly is very important but of course, children still have their own individual approaches to learning and a teacher needs to be aware of this too in order to teach effectively

Effective teaching should emphasise that there is rarely a single 'right' method for solving a problem. This allows for personalised learning to some extent, as the children can use methods they are most comfortable with.

The highest levels of achievement have been found to be in classes where teachers have a good knowledge of students' achievement as well as a wide range of teaching approaches (Peterson et al., 1989, pp. 559). Herein rests the rationale for assessment, which informs a teacher's understanding of where a child is up to in his or her understanding of the subject matter and in so doing is fundamental for children's progression. There are widely recognised differences in the way in which high attainers and low attainers solve problems in mathematics. It would seem that successful problem solvers have a range of strategies that they use intensively in problem solving, above and beyond the mathematical content that they know. These would include, checking that they have understood the problem, planning their approach and monitoring their progress towards their goal.

Just as competence in early number relies on a blending of 'knowing that' and 'figuring out', improving competence at mathematical problem-solving involves increasing both the fund of mathematical knowledge and a range

146

of general strategies, which have developed together (Askew, 1992, pp. 25). In the context of the National Curriculum for Mathematics, this would suggest that learning outcomes, which focus on separate attainment targets are less likely to be successful than those that require students to integrate ideas from two attainment targets. In terms of progression, this means that teaching needs to provide activities that focus on the links between different aspects of mathematics rather than treating them as separate topics and this is something I have always strived to achieve in my own teaching.

As assessment is able to inform a teacher's planning, different children's needs are accommodated. This allows the teacher to adapt teaching according to the individual child and often is accompanied by setting arrangements. Many schools employ setting for mathematics more than any other subject as an organisational device for coping with the range of competencies within a year group. The popularity of setting for mathematics reflects recognition by teachers that mathematics spreads students out in terms of their competencies more than any subject in the school curriculum. Furthermore, it is often the case that the lowest set consists of a smaller number of students than the others. Haylock (1992, pp. 10) points out that this itself is recognition of the idiosyncratic nature of low attainment in mathematics and the consequent need for much individual attention by the teacher for those students in these lower sets.

Evidence presented by Allan (1991, pp. 61) states that mathematical attainment groupings can lead to some gains in attainment and although setting can be a contentious issue, there is little evidence to suggest students can be harmed by attainment grouping. For students with special educational needs (SEN), Stuard (1990, pp. 21) makes the valid point that they should not be put in situations where they fail, but should be given opportunities to display what they can do, without recording or verbalising. This should help them in their confidence, as they progress to the next level in their understanding of a concept or topic.

As well as using extra teaching staff to enhance learning objectives, ICT can be extremely effective. Beardon (2003, pp. 157) refers to examples of how technology as a tool for learning can accommodate different learning styles, since allowing children to use computers as mathematical tools can encourage them to have an input into the direction of inquiries or investigations so that different interests, learning styles and preferences are taken into account. The evidence presented by Bearden suggests that when the teacher permits real child-centred learning in this way, hidden abilities and creativity can be uncovered and mathematical concept development and thinking often go well beyond the expected outcome. Additionally, by opening up communications with the wider learning community, the Internet has helped to radically change schools by giving them free access not only to information richer than any school library but also to other schools, expert advice and online resources.

In my personal experience of teaching, I frequently used the Internet as a means for obtaining useful ideas, worksheets and resources in which to aid children's progression in their understanding of mathematics. Any mention of technology within the context of mathematics should not overlook the impact of calculators. The National Curriculum in the UK requires the use of the calculator in Key Stage 1 and Key Stage 2, as there are many benefits to the use of calculators. For example, children of 6 or 7 can explore the 'constant' facility of the calculator, and derive patterns by counting on in twos or threes. Stuard (1990, pp. 10) also makes the point that the use of calculates encourages children to work with large numbers, negative numbers and decimals, and to discuss these ideas with other children and adults. I remember in a Year 5 lesson for example, giving students the chance to learn about the calculator's memory function, which implicitly is highly useful for providing an effective means for enabling children to cope with the notion of 'structural limitation', discussed earlier. Calculators therefore provide a fundamental tool with which to both encourage and help children develop in their mathematical understanding.

Once resources such as ICT, calculators and teaching staff are appropriately in place, considerable effort is required by the teacher to then structure the class into groups, which will work effectively together. This is because many studies have shown that students may be working in groups but not working as a group (Askew, 1992, pp.'36), which has serious implications for children's progression. Research presented by Webb (1984, pp. 34)

148

suggests that the optimum grouping would comprise of 'near' mixed ability groups such as high and middle attainers or middle and low attainers as well as mixed sex groups, which include balanced numbers of boys and girls. Particular focus on grouping arrangements needs to be made if there are children with English as an additional language (EAL) in the classroom. This is because it is often the case according to Askew (1992, Pp. 61) that poor language skills – reading, writing, and speaking – are associated with low attainment in mathematics. Given the point made by Brown (1989, pp. 40) that through carrying out work in a social setting, group work promotes learning, it is easy to see how children with EAL would benefit from working in mixed groups of native English-speaking children.

To be involved in mathematics, at whatever level, requires both content and process, in order for the subject to be experienced in a balanced way. For children's progression in their understanding of mathematics to be realised therefore, effective teaching is needed, which accommodates students with different needs and abilities. This requires good planning, making use of exercises and activities children enjoy. Enjoyment is most likely to be achieved if mathematics is placed in 'real' contexts that the children would have come across in their everyday experience and in this respect, it is good discipline for teachers of mathematics to evaluate tasks given to students against the criterion of usefulness. However, a productive dialogue between the teacher and students in which the teacher uses statements and questions, which, as children progress, increasingly requires them to verbalise understanding of their working, should underpin this criterion. It is in this way that misconceptions can be more frequently addressed, enabling children to progress in their conceptual development.

Both formative and summative assessment data should be used to record these misconceptions and inform planning in terms of where children are up to in their understanding of a topic or concept. Teaching can then be appropriately differentiated to offer more personalised learning that meets a diverse range of needs and abilities, including' children with SEN and children with EAL as well as Gifted & Talented children. Careful attention needs to be paid by the teacher to the grouping arrangements to allow for maximum learning, since it is by such processes of social interaction and dialogue with more experienced learners that children learn to be reflective about their own processing and so begin to learn how to learn. Likewise, effective uses of resources, including technology and teaching assistants is important for helping children further develop this meta-awareness and control, which ultimately, is fundamental in enabling children to progress in becoming increasingly independent learners.

25. Flipped Learning

Flipped learning is a pedagogical model in which the teacher delivery during in-class time is flipped with the homework elements of a course. As a type of blended learning technique, students can watch relevant videos at home, which have been prepared by the teacher, while using in-class time to focus on their exercises, projects or discussions.

My own transition to a flipped learning classroom was a gradual, organic process. For occasional lessons with older students (10 years and over), I have come to recognise the many advantages of a flipped learning model. Sharing relevant tutorial videos with students and colleagues, both from my own YouTube channel and links elsewhere on the Web, has enabled me to spend more time as a facilitator of learning. This simply means that learners spend less time passively listening at the beginning of the lesson and more time engaged in activities. By doing away with the traditional classroom, which can be very teacher centred, it has also enabled me to spend extra time providing valuable one-on-one assistance to students who need it the most.

According to Eric Sheninger (2016), author of Uncommon Learning, there are two main components associated with the flipped learning approach:

1. *Students watch lectures and consume other forms of content outside of school at their own pace whilst communicating with peers and teachers using online learning tools.* From my own experience, this point about students working at their own pace should be kept in mind. The ability for students to pause, rewind and fast-forward a tutorial video means that they are in a much better situation to assimilate new learning.

2. *Students apply what they have learnt during in class time with assistance from the teacher.* As there is more time freed up during the lesson itself, there are more opportunities for small-group work and one-to-one contact with lower-performing students.

In order to make the lesson time itself more engaging while integrating opportunities formative assessment, there are many web-based tools that can complement the students' main in class activities, which I have found to be useful:

Animoto – this tool helps you to create professional looking slide shows. All you need to do is attach some photos and add background music.

Padlet – this is like a giant noticeboard and allows learners to write a short message and/or attach an image on the 'wall' for others to see. These messages can then be moved around just like Post-it notes, and in the same way as with Google Docs, learners can collaborate on the same project together. As well as a medium in which to record work digitally, I have found it especially useful for school trips. The application is great for when students take their own devices and can quickly upload their photos following a trip to a museum, for example.

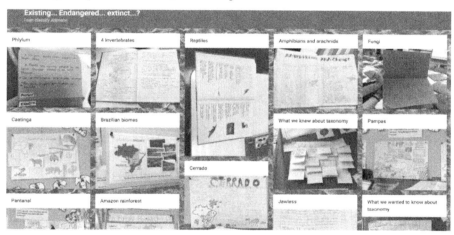

Plickers – This assessment tool allows teachers to quickly collect formative assessment data without the need to have students use devices or paper and pencil.

Kahoot – This is a game-based learning platform that allows the teacher to create multiple-choice quizzes. It is a favourite with our teachers and students, as it can easily be used to review students' knowledge, for formative assessment, or as a break from traditional classroom activities.

In addition, there are also some fantastic tools out there for students themselves to become authors, teachers and collaborators, working together to teach content to each other. Three of my favourite tools for students to use are listed here (with links to tutorial videos on how each tool can be used):

Adobe Spark (*previously 'Adobe Voice'*) (https://www.youtube.com/watch?v=vKYVIM5uAJk)

VideoScribe (https://www.youtube.com/watch?v=dqUfUKlf-go)

Explain Everything (https://youtu.be/3Fjf75EhRTU)

A Glance at Google Apps for Education

Google's free suite of online tools are now widely used by students and teachers all over the world. My experience with this suite of online tools is that it makes a very significant contribution to social constructivist learning. **Social constructivism** is the idea that learners construct their own mental models, and these models develop through collaboration with others.

The concept of *social* constructivism began from the work of psychologists, namely Lev Vygotsky and Jerome Bruner. Vygotsky came up with the idea he referred to as the **'zone of proximal development'** – the notion that there is an area of activity just a little bit beyond what a child can already do – it is what they can do with help. As we saw earlier, Bruner gave educators the analogy of **'scaffolding'** the new skills that the child was learning, by

152

providing support and guidance to get to the next point.

Google Apps for Education not only makes these elements of social constructivism possible, but it actively promotes this type of pedagogy. One of the most important benefits is that several users can work on a project from different computers – synchronously or asynchronously. In my experience, this gives a feeling of shared ownership and collaborative effort, helping to increase student motivation. The document shown here is an example of a 4th grade (Year 5) group project in which groups of three students work as a team to research and answer the following questions about oil.

Task:

Answer the following three questions, using the links below to help you.

1. Where in the world do we get our oil from? *(Show on a World Map)*

2. How is oil found?

3. How is oil formed?

4. Which items are made from or use oil, plastic, nylon, polyester and glycerine.
   - http://media.ft.com/cms/19d4f43e-a1a5-11dc-a13b-0000779fd2ac.swf
     - The Financial Times website hosts this interactive map showing oil producers, consumers and oil movement.From Fieldwork Education
   - http://oils.gpa.unep.org/kids/kids.htm
     - The Global Marine Pollution Information Gateway is a children's site, with helpful information on a number of themes related to this unit.
   - http://awesome.good.is/transparency/web/1005/oil-consumption/flash.html
     - An excellent visual reference, showing oil consumption and production.
   - www.guardian.co.uk/news/datablog/2010/jun/09/bp-energystatistics-consumption-reserves-energy#
     - The Guardian website features an article on oil consumption, accompanied by an informative visual diagram that can be enlarged.

It is easy to see what each individual student contributes to a document like this because Google Docs assigns every contributor a unique colour. My advice though, would be to keep the groups working on the same document small. You do not really want too many students working on the same document because it does become difficult to disentangle who has made which changes, and as with any online collaborative tool, it simply becomes more of a challenge to coordinate who should be doing what.

In small online working groups, it is also easier to keep track of different comments made on the work by others. This brings another benefit of Google documents, which is the ability to add comments on the side of the work. To insert a comment, highlight the text, then choose Insert a Comment under the Insert Menu. You just highlight some text in the body of the document and the comment will appear on the right side of the page.

It is basically a digital post-it note on the side of the document. Click on any comment and watch the highlighted text in the document change colour to quickly pinpoint the suggested revision. Comments are clever and they disappear after the issue has been addressed by the author so students feel a sense of accomplishment as they work their way through the suggestions of their peers. I would also say that students are more likely to revisit their work if they know someone else will be commenting on it.

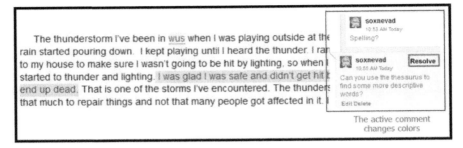

This feature of comments can be particularly good for documents shared just between a teacher and student – the teacher can use the comments to bring the student's attention to mistakes, and to facilitate a form of scaffold questions to improve the student's writing.

The comments also remove barriers between writers and further creates a sense of class community. In addition, Docs provide support for collaboration in real time so students and teachers can have a virtual mini-conference about the work in front of them from any location if the timing is right. This can be done by instant messaging chat, in which users shared into the document can chat synchronously about their project. By adding this synchronous communication medium into the tool, it also gives a feeling of social presence, which adds to student engagement.

These features of Google Docs give rise to what I consider to be the most valuable of all pedagogical benefits – **small group work**. By producing the conditions of small group work, concepts, skills and attitudes such as cooperation, collaboration and rational argument can be developed. Exploring and valuing the contributions of others is excellent preparation for life in a culturally diverse society. According to the ideas of Brown, Barnfield & Stone (1990), small group work can lead to:

– a secure environment that some less confident students need in order to express their ideas;

– some children accepting responsibility to help others;

– full involvement of all the children in the task;

154

– children recognising the contributions of others as important as their own; and,

– children being able to recognise the individuality of others.

Small group work that is facilitated through the use of Google Docs naturally leads students to pool their ideas, listen to each other and to have respect for each person's contributions to the work of the group.

When students are at the planning stage of an assignment, they can use a tool like Draw.io (which is integrated into the Google Apps suite) to make mind maps and do collaborative brainstorming. The asynchronous nature of digital brainstorming sessions provides all students with an opportunity to contribute, unlike traditional brainstorming sessions which encourage contributions from the "quick thinkers" in the room. Students can use shapes, arrows, text, and imported images to build a visual map for any task. Again, the revision history uses colours to highlight and track changes, making it easy to see what each student has contributed to the big picture.

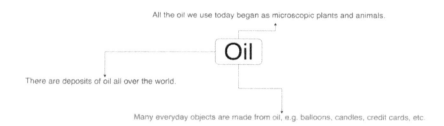

All the oil we use today began as microscopic plants and animals.

Oil

There are deposits of oil all over the world.

Many everyday objects are made from oil, e.g. balloons, candles, credit cards, etc.

Another big advantage for students and teachers is the use of templates. You can provide students with a starting point for digital writing by creating templates. This saves time and guides the learning by giving students a consistent page format which can include links, images and directions, all helping to jump start the learning. All you have to do is just create a Google Doc and then save it as a template. Students can pick up a copy of a template and instantly store it in their own list of Google Docs. The Google Sheet below is a brilliant example of a template for a maths project in which students need to complete the information about regular polygons.

File   Edit   View   Insert   Format   Data   Tools   Add-ons   Help   All changes saved in Drive

🖶 ↶ ↷ 🖶 | $ % 0 .00 123 ▾ | Arial   ▾ | 12   ▾ | B I S A ▾ ◇ ▾ ⊞ ▾ ⊡ ▾ | ≡ ▾

Name of Shape

	A	B	C	D	E	F	G	H
	Name of Shape	Drawing	No .of Sides	Length of each side (cm)	Size of each Angle	Total of all Angles	Reflective Symmetry	Order of Rotational Symmetry
	Equilateral Triangle	▲	3	7	60°	180°	3	3
	Square	☐						
	Pentagon	⬠						
	Hexagon	⬡						
	Heptagon	⬡						

+ ▤   Sheet1 ▾

As well as giving my students opportunities to use these tools, I have used each one of these applications myself as a medium in which to share information with students for them to learn at their own pace. As Sheninher himself states though, 'pedagogy always trumps technology'. For digital learning to be implemented effectively, the focus should be on pedagogy first and technology second. When integrating technology, it must be remembered that it is less about the tool and more about what students can do with the tools handed to them.

That being said, with all these web-based tools and other digital applications available, it makes sense that a Bring Your Own Device (BYOD) or 1:1 technology initiative can radically enhance the flipped learning model. By providing students with access to their own device, it can bring out the best of what flipped learning has to offer. According to Sheninger (2016, pp. 117),

The flipped classroom is an excellent first step in making students' in-class experiences more active, more student centred, and more meaningful. Combining the best aspects of the flipped classroom with the power of 1:1 technology would allow for an even more radical reshaping of the classroom. School should become a place where students can learn at their own individual paces, become active creators instead of solely passive content recipients, and learn in an environment that they "own", which adjusts rapidly to meet their learning

156

needs and interests.

26. Developing Students' Digital Literacy Skills

With all the focus schools have on digital technology use, it is important that students develop their digital literacy, to use these tools appropriately and responsibly. For schools using Google Apps for Education, a free online project-based video curriculum has been created to help teach and learn practical digital skills.

1. Go to the Applied Digital Skills site and sign up.

2. Once you're signed up as a teacher, you can share with your students the self-paced lessons via your Google Classroom. I have picked out these links below, which are particularly useful for helping students to develop their online research and presentation skills using Google Apps for Education:

Research and Develop a Topic

Create a Presentation All About a Topic

Organise Files in Drive

Create a Photo Journal in Google Docs

The Common Sense Media site for educators (https://www.commonsense.org/education/) also has access to a range of relevant resources and lesson plans for teaching students about digital literacy and citizenship. If you work with younger students (5 to 11 years), you may find my first book particularly helpful, *Computing and ICT Lessons for the Primary School* in which you can find dedicated lesson plans for E-Safety and Digital Citizenship for across the primary-age range.

27. BYOD

Bring Your Own Device (BYOD) refers to the trend in which students/employees bring their own mobile technologies (usually smartphones) into their place of work or study. BYOD has become increasingly common in recent years owing to the fact that mobile technologies with access to the Internet are now both more affordable and more ubiquitous than ever. Given the immense potential for learning opportunities made possible by smartphones and other Internet-connected devices, it is only logical to harness and leverage this technology in order to enrich students' learning. Improvements in WiFi access has therefore led many educational institutions to implement a clear roadmap for a BYOD initiative. In pursuit of successful teaching, this is absolutely necessary. Along with suggestions put forward by Eric Sheninger (2016) in his book, *Uncommon Learning*, I share here some of my thoughts and experiences about what makes a BYOD initiative successful:

1. **Clear Vision & Plan** – As Sheninger points out, a consistent focus on student learning and sound pedagogy should be central to any BYOD initiative. This means that all stakeholders must be on the same page when it comes to having a shared rationale, goals and expectations surrounding BYOD. Assemblies, PTA meetings and discussions with the Board of Governors, all provide excellent opportunities to communicate what a BYOD initiative means for the school. In particular, teachers also need support and guidance through professional development workshops, which help them to make the most of BYOD to develop pedagogically sound lessons. In my own experience, this sort of professional development should be ongoing even after the BYOD initiative has begun.

2. **Sound Policy** – According to Sheninger, a sound policy addresses Wi-Fi login procedures, a focus on learning, acceptable use, and absolving the school of any liability for lost, stolen, or broken devices. It's also worthwhile getting students involved with this. For example, I enlisted the help of our Digital Leaders to put together a tutorial video to show all their peers about how to install the school's CA security certificate.

3. **Infrastructure** – The IT service team needs to be up to speed on the BYOD initiative and the school's network should be ready to withstand all of the mobile technologies connecting to it. This is pivotal to ensuring the smooth running of the BYOD initiative.

4. **Relevant Applications** – The applications that I referenced for Flipped Learning can also effectively be utilised as part of a BYOD initiative.

Where they can be usefully integrated into lessons, getting students to install augmented reality apps like HP Reveal (see Part Four, 'Educational Resources' for more information) onto their own devices, can also help to create engaging and memorable lessons.

With the emergence of Google Cardboard and accompanying apps like Discovery VR, you can go further still, by making perfect use of students' devices for the creation of virtual reality experiences. If used well, these can really enhance lessons by bringing to life the subject of study.

5. **Technology Events** – A technology event or week is a great way to launch a BYOD initiative at your school. Lastly, raising awareness of what we actually have available to us in terms of Internet-connected mobile device technology, how it should be used and how it can be used to facilitate learning, is very important. In addition to running assemblies and events related to Digital Citizenship and E-Safety, an annual Technology Week is a great way to get both teachers and students involved in maximising the use of their mobile devices to enhance teaching & learning.

Exemplar letters to send to parents about BYOD:

Dear Parents,

Next week we will be celebrating our Upper Primary Technology Week. Among the various activities we have organised, students in Class 3, 4 and 5 are also invited to bring their mobile devices (smartphones) into school. This is part of our BYOD (Bring Your Own Device) initiative, which is now common in many schools around the world, to support students' learning. Obviously, not all students will have their own personal devices to bring into school and in these instances, a school iPad will be provided.

In preparation for this event, all students have been provided a **BYOD form** *for you to read through at home with your child and sign. The form outlines the school's expectations of students who use their mobile device in school, and it must be returned in order for your child to be allowed to use his or her personal device whilst in school. Additionally, when students come into school with their devices, they must install the school security CA certificate, which keeps their phone safe (by blocking inappropriate sites) if and when surfing the web at school.*

*In order to get the most out of Technology Week and future BYOD activities, we recommend that students install the following apps (***all free***) on their iPhones (equivalent or similar apps can be found in the Android store):*

Adobe Spark

Aurasma

Cooltour VR

Discovery VR

Google Classroom

Google Drive

iMovie

Kahoot

Quizlet

Spacecraft 3D

Stop Motion Studio

We will begin by introducing students to Virtual Reality (VR) next week, which will give them an opportunity to use our VR headsets to experience a virtual field trip! **For this activity next week therefore, students should install the Cooltour VR and Discovery VR apps.** *The other educational apps are recommended, but not necessary to enjoy all of the activities planned for next week. As with all other BYOD activities, students will only be permitted to use their mobile devices in school as and when directed by their teacher.*

If you have any doubts or questions about the BYOD initiative for this year's Technology Week, please do not hesitate to get in touch.

160

Kind regards,

Mr Will

....

Most parents will be supportive of a BYOD initiative. However, as with any new initiative there will always be some parents who show resistance – the email here from one of the mothers is a case in point.

Dear Mr Will,

A lot of C3 students don't have a smartphone – which I think is positive.

When the school asks to bring their mobile I think it makes the ones that don't have it feel uncomfortable. My son does not have one and asked to take mine which is not possible as I only have one.

He could take an iPad but he said it was only an iPhone/smartphone. Is this correct?

I think you should reconsider this activity next time for C3 students or suggest they take the phone or the iPad.

Thank you,

Jane

....

Dear Jane,

Thank you for your email. The spirit of this activity is simply to harness the power of mobile technologies for students' learning. There is no expectation for students to have their own device and those without their own device can use a school iPad. For students who do have their own device, this can be a smartphone, iPad or even a laptop – all of the apps listed (or equivalents) are accessible on all types of mobile device. Some students, if they have a choice about which device to bring, may prefer to bring a smartphone (if they have one) because of the extra portability – but this is not necessary.

I hope this helps to clarify the BYOD initiative as part of Technology Week. However, if you have any further concerns, or would like me to have a chat with your son, please let me know.

Kind regards,

Mr Will

As much as possible, you should do your best to alleviate parents' concerns. Some parents quite rightly will be worried that their children already spend too much time on screen-based devices. This is where teaching children about digital citizenship comes in; any BYOD initiative launched successfully in schools will make sure that students learn to use their devices *appropriately and responsibly*, for the benefit of their learning. Moreover, successful digital citizenship education also involves the parents.

To summarise, the following points should be made clear to parents about BYOD:

1. There is no expectation for their child to own a device or bring a device.

2. The devices belonging to students can only be used at the teacher's request.

3. The devices are only to be used to support learning.

4. Students receive digital citizenship and e-safety lessons to ensure that they use their devices appropriately and responsibly.

28. Genius Hour

Genius Hour is an enquiry-based learning process. As a student-directed learning model, it is intended to give students the opportunity to explore their own interests while developing their knowledge, skills and understanding.

The idea for Genius Hour was originally started by Google, in which it allowed its engineers to spend 20% of their work time on their own passion projects. Many of Google's services such as Gmail and Google News are thanks to its policy of having Genius Hour.

By allowing time for students to study topics they are curious about, Genius Hour can be seen to encourage students' creativity and motivation, while paving the way for them to become lifelong learners. The workshop style of Genius Hour, in which collaboration is encouraged, should also benefit students' social skills and confidence.

Wentzel & Wigfield (1998) for example, found that offering students appropriate choices relating to the content and process of learning has been shown to provide a sense of control over outcomes and is associated with increased levels of motivation and achievement. Below is a suggested guideline for introducing greater student autonomy and independent learning through Genius Hour:

Genius Hour Guidelines

There are **five key steps** for students to follow:

1. Pick a topic.

2. Develop an enquiry question.

3. Do the research.

4. Present what you have learnt.

5. Reflect.

Refer to the Appendix for relevant Genius Hour resources, which can be used with students.

29. Developing News Literacy

For most readers of this book, the term 'news literacy' is probably an unfamiliar one. However, for the purpose of *Successful Teaching for Everyone*, news literacy has become increasingly important area of digital citizenship that ought to be taught. Irrespective of whether or not your school curriculum will be adapted to explicitly incorporate this area in the future, news literacy is a subject that the individual teacher (whatever his or her subject specialism), should teach. Moreover, for cultivating the increasingly used buzz word, 'international-mindedness', news literacy can prove surprisingly useful.

Before I go any further, if you already have an understanding of news literacy and its importance, you may simply just want a useful resource to use with students rather than a thorough explanation of the subject (which will follow). If this is the case for you, I recommend that you subscribe to The Sift (https://newslit.org/educators/sift/), which is an online resource to help teachers and students sharpen their news literacy skills.

Please note, this section is most relevant for teachers of older students (from 9 years up) but can serve as useful reference for all teachers.

The global news landscape has changed dramatically in recent years. News readership has increasingly shifted to the Internet because of inexpensive technology, ubiquitous access and free content. This has led to a trend of information democratisation in which information control has shifted from a few powerful entities toward smaller outlets and individual citizens. User-generated news sources like blogs, wiki pages and YouTube videos are now commonplace. As a result, according to the Pew Research Center (2012), the audience for news on the Internet has grown from nothing in 1993 to second behind only television.

Although the Internet brings users more news, there is consequently more uncertainty about whether news sources – both traditional and otherwise – are providing relevant or even credible information. Powers (2010, pp. 5), for example, states that young people in particular, report being overwhelmed by the amount of news sources and content available online. This makes it increasingly important for news consumers to develop digital literacy skills that allow them to weigh the value of what they read, see, and hear.

News literacy, a fundamental yet too often unrecognised area of digital literacy, helps students to foster a more intellectually rigorous relationship with news media. News literacy is neatly defined by Schwarz (2011, pp. 1) as 'the reader's ability to critically evaluate, interpret and process as well as participate in news media'. As we live in an increasingly interconnected and globalised world, I would argue that the word "global" should also be used when discussing news literacy; much of the news content viewed online is from international journalism networks, which create what Reese (2012) refers to as a "global news arena". Reese explains that bringing a global perspective to news literacy requires a basic awareness of how national contexts differ; it means taking concrete local circumstances into account while being aware of how they differ from other areas and how global forces bring "influence from a distance".

Global news is a highly complex, albeit important subject. Having worked in two bilingual British schools, one in El Salvador and the other in Brazil, I have seen the importance of this subject manifest in the overall objectives of the International Primary Curriculum (IPC) and International Baccalaureate (IB). These programmes correctly consider themselves to be leading proponents of international education and are designed to promote international mindedness (Stagg, 2013). Students on the IB for example, are required to keep up-to-date with current national and international news events relevant to their areas of study. Moreover, "international mindedness" is one of the key traits and values of many schools, encouraging students to develop a cosmopolitan attitude and willingness to

164

learn about life in other parts of the world. All of this forms part of the Council of International Schools (CIS) accreditation process, which asks schools to 'demonstrate a commitment to internationalism in education' (CIS, 2013).

Unfortunately, despite the buzz words in the curriculum and the rhetoric of schools, little is actually done to facilitate learning about the world in which we live. Specifically, the most relevant sources for informing students (and their teachers) about social, economic and political events happening around the world – global news media – are widely absent from the classroom. This seems to be the case in educational institutions around the world (Stagg, 2013; Schwarz, 2012; Buckingham, 2003).

The media has three main functions: to inform, guide, and entertain. It is generally agreed, however, that media's most important role is to tell the public what is going on in the world and why. This in turn gives us the definition for news itself, which according to Smith (2007, pp. 13) is to 'tell its audience something it doesn't already know'. There may be nothing they can do about it, says Smith, but they need this information to make the choices necessary in a democratic society. The argument for news literacy education therefore, rests on the premise that news media is fundamental to democracy. Altschull (1990) refers to this belief as the democratic assumption:

'The decisions made by people in the voting booths are based on information made available to them. The information is provided mainly by the news media. Hence, the news media are indispensable to the survival of democracy'.

This gives the news a very distinct and important role, setting it well apart from other media content. It is important, according to Ashley et al. (2013, pp. 7), to distinguish news literacy from the broader and more widely used term media literacy; unlike other media content, the news plays a crucial role in safeguarding democratic societies and democratic citizenship. This is because the news media provides the primary source of information about political, economic and societal affairs, helping citizens to form opinions that cover a wide range of issues affecting choices about governments and policies. It is the job of reporters then to gather the news, check its accuracy, and present it in a way that can interest and be understood by the public.

Although relevant as a framework to understanding rights, freedoms, and claims for better quality information in a pluralistic society, the conception of news and democracy, according to Mihailidis (2011), is overly idealised, and this is why news literacy education matters so much. Certainly, on a global scale, national biases exist, in which significant stories about countries elsewhere in the world may be ignored, as they are not perceived to be 'relevant' in the parochial eyes of the mainstream news media. Writing apropos of television and daily newspapers for example, Hamelink (1976, pp. 120) interprets the news as a functional element of hegemony, pushing the views of the dominant interests of society.

'… "information about the world" is presented in incoherent fragments (especially in "newscasts") or in pre-digested explanations which can only be passively filed away. In this way "information" functions as an oppressive tool since, by its manner of presentation, it keeps people from shaping their own world. The incoherent fragments preclude the wholistic perspective which enables insight into the interdependence between happenings, into the involvement of one's own context, and into the possibility of acting upon the challenge thus posed'.

Hamelink suggests that the only way people can have a chance to intervene in their reality is for information channels to be created that permit the coherent organisation of information. News literacy, thus, would be promoted by giving readers a clearer insight into why news providers are 'pushing' particular stories over others. From the perspective of the global news arena, this means national biases could be overcome if only the information channels themselves change. To this end, one might expect that the free flow of information facilitated by the Internet has led to a well-informed citizenry able to pressure governments and journalists for more transparency. The highly acclaimed media scholar, Marshall McLuhan (1964, pp. 5), even predicted as much:

'Increased speed of communication and the ability of people to read about, spread, and react to global news quickly, forces us to become more involved with one another from various social groups and countries around the world and to be more aware of our global responsibilities'.

Despite the seemingly endless possibilities for knowledge transfer presented by the Internet, the reality is something quite different from what McLuhan had envisaged. This is because the sheer quantity of information available and its ease of access has led to what Whitworth (2009, pp. 4) has referred to as information obesity, in which 'Information is not being turned into knowledge and then fed back into the environment to be drawn on later'. For example, more information with no objective value whatsoever has been made available by the Internet. Thomspon (2008) refers to such

166

information as 'counterknowledge', which he defines as "misinformation packaged to look like fact". In the context of news online, this issue is particularly pertinent since anyone can become a citizen journalist and post "news" online. Although this gives news consumers substantial choice and control over their news diet, it becomes problematic if news consumers take everything they read, see or hear at face value. In an online world circulating great quantities of information, it becomes more difficult to find international news that is reliable, high-quality and relevant to the pressing issues facing the world.

However, even putting the ideals behind global news literacy to one side, there is still plenty of value in using the news to improve literacy standards in schools. Studies consistently show that newspaper reading contributes to reading and writing skill development (Palmer et al., 1994, pp. 51). According to Bernadowski (2011, pp. 5), the newspaper is the perfect textbook for so-called 'adolescent literacy', because it is written at a level that many of them can read, and it provides adolescents with much needed skills and strategies to function in the adult world. Moreover, Phelps & Pottorff (1992, pp. 2) state that newspapers provide special elements that have been well received by secondary students with reading problems. For example, comprehension can be fostered by introducing the journalistic approach to news reporting and semantics can be taught by helping students discover the meaning of new words through context. Given the broader cultural and educational value of using the news in education, there should be a greater effort made to include it in school curricula.

In his book, The Filter Bubble, Pariser (2011) describes a digital situation we all now face in which website algorithms selectively present information to users based on location, click behaviour, search history, etc., and, as a result, distance users from information that disagrees with their viewpoints, effectively isolating them in their own cultural or ideological bubbles. In December 2009, for example, Google began using 57 different signals – everything from a user login location to their browser to their search history – to make guesses about who the user is and what kinds of sites the user would like to see. Likewise, social networking sites such a Facebook and Twitter are built on the premise that users interact with other users that they have chosen to interact with, which limits the coverage of news they receive. Although filter bubbles almost certainly provide users with information of subjective value, based on their needs, desires and preferences, they also lead users to a state of cognitive bias. This means users may dismiss otherwise potentially useful information, because it does not conform to their cognitive schema. As more users discover news through algorithm-determined feeds, important news content relevant to the public sphere falls out of view.

According Pariser (2011, pp. 4): *'Democracy requires citizens to see things from one another's point of view, but instead we're more and more enclosed in our own bubbles'.*

In order to be news literate on a global scale, it is surely necessary to break out of these filter bubbles by reading from a wider variety of sources from around the world.

Another type of filter bubble can be seen in terms of the coverage of global news itself. Reese (2011, pp. 5) states that against the expectation that media report and reach the entire globe, the global media system, particularly international broadcasting, does not live up to that hope. For example, Alisa Miller, head of Public Radio International, presented a cartogram during a TED Conference to show how the US media covers international news.

Fig. 1

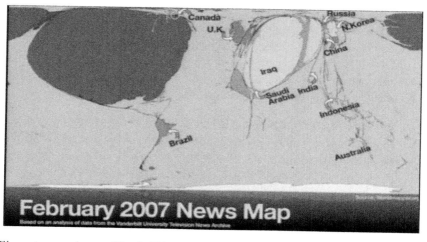

The cartogram shows a filter bubble in US TV broadcast news distribution in 2007.

This map shown in Figure 1 represents the number of seconds US network and cable news organisations dedicated to news stories by country in February 2007. This was a month when there had been very significant international events: North Korea agreed to dismantle its nuclear facilities, there was massive flooding in Indonesia, and the Intergovernmental Panel on Climate Change (IPCC) released a study confirming man's impact on

168

global warming. During this month though, Miller (2007) observes the US accounted for 79% of the total news coverage; the combined coverage of China, India, and Russia represented just 1% of the news. Similar distortions in the way news is covered can be seen in elite online newspapers such as the New York Times and Guardian.

What the cartogram serves to illustrate is that, contrary to what people might think, news media does not deliver an equitable distribution of global news coverage. According to Adams and Ovide (2009), the online availability of news and the demand for larger corporate profits has driven both audiences and advertisers to cyberspace, triggering a crisis in the news industry, which is increasingly turning to local coverage. Consequently, foreign news bureaus have been disappearing, as foreign correspondents are seen at best as unnecessary "middle men", at worst as "endangered species". (Hamilton, 2009, pp. 463).

Fig. 2

Bias of domestic news readership on domestic news sites

As Figure 2 illustrates, the same problem can be seen on the demand side for news. On average, more than 95% of national news readership is on domestic sites. Citizens in the UK, for example, are unlikely to read about news happening in Australia on an Australian website. Instead, they are far more likely to read about events in Australia, filtered through a UK news outlet, such as the Guardian. Language can be an obvious barrier here, preventing readers from visiting foreign news sites. With relatively high numbers of immigrants, this may explain why the US and UK have comparatively more of their citizens viewing foreign web pages than China,

169

for instance, which has proportionally fewer immigrants.

Nonetheless, the fact that the vast majority of page views are on domestic news sites for all countries is considered by Zuckerman (2010) to be a serious problem:

'The real problems in the world are global in scale and scope; they require conversations to get to global solutions. This is a problem we have to solve'.

Moreover, when foreign news is reported by a domestic outlet, true comparative analysis is rare. News, according to Reese (2012, pp. 2), is 'still domesticated through national frames of references, often taken for granted, and media globalisation skeptics have argued that no truly transnational news platforms have emerged, permitting the kind of cross-boundary dialogs associate with a public sphere'. Media sceptics such as Hafez (2007) point to the continued weaknesses of international reporting: 'elite-focused, conflict-based, and driven by scandal and the sensational, leading them to conclude that the "global village" has been blocked by domestication'.

As so much of our news now comes from online sources, we need to ensure that our students have the digital literacy skills needed in order to become well-informed global citizens. If they lack these skills, then we cannot truly claim to be providing an education that facilitates the often touted ideal of "international mindedness".

What are the barriers to the inclusion of news literacy in school curricula?

Technology has made the world increasingly interconnected, but not necessarily better informed. One of the key roles of technology today should be to help learners better understand the world we live in, and this means teaching news literacy in schools. Yet despite some efforts by those championing media and news literacy, Gretchen Schwarz (2006, pp. 255) writes that its proponents are still dealing with 'all the problems of a young field – becoming visible in the academic world, acquiring credibility among educators and others, developing a strong research basis, and finding funding'.

The challenges facing media literacy education become even more pronounced when one looks specifically at its subset, news literacy education.

As media scholar, Fifi Schwarz (2012, pp. 1) points out,

'The most relevant sources for informing citizens about social, economic & political affairs – news media – are often overlooked in media literacy education. This seems rather odd, considering that interest in news media among (young) citizens clearly relates to their civic engagement'.

Similarly, media educator David Buckingham (2003, pp. 3) writes,

'It is quite extraordinary that the majority of young people should go through their school careers with so little opportunity to study and engage with the most significant contemporary forms of culture and communication. Clearly, there is an argument here that still needs to be made'.

There are several possible reasons why news literacy has received little scholarly attention and has been underrepresented in education curricula. First and foremost, news literacy has been overshadowed by the more popular subject, media literacy. Schwarz (2012, pp. 2) suggests this is to do with the fact that news media is generally associated with, or falls into the category of what he refers to as "old media", which is not as popular with young people, especially in the digital age. Buckingham (2000, pp. 9) supports this claim with data, reporting that young people frequently express indifference, or even considerable dislike, towards the news. This is a significant point given the underlying philosophy of media education in general as a form of inoculation. Buckingham (2003, pp. 19) explains that this idea comes from the belief that students should be partly exposed to the debilitating forms of media influence in the classroom so as to ultimately enhance their immunity from manipulation. In terms of news media however, this notion of inoculation can be seen to not apply – after all, it does not make sense to spend time teaching students news literacy in order to "inoculate" them if they are not interested in news itself. For this reason, other areas of media literacy education have held greater importance in the eyes of educators.

As an ephemeral and potentially contentious subject, news by its very nature can also be seen as a difficult, if not an unnecessary media, to bring into the classroom. Laufenberg (2010) states that:

'There is tons of news out there, and you need to interact with it at an analytic level as it happens. You cannot plan ahead for current events, and it makes some teachers uncomfortable to plan lessons around things that have not yet happened. They want to control the content'.

Hobbs (2010, pp. 7) adds to this point by suggesting that, 'where competition and fragmentation of news audiences reign, no easy assumptions can be made about the nature of what counts as trustworthy and authoritative when it comes to news and current events'.

The result is that however relevant or useful it might be, most teachers are reluctant to use the news as part of their daily pedagogy. This situation is not helped of course, by the fact that there is no training given to teachers on how to teach news literacy. Hobbs (2004, pp. 53) writes that:

'Based on my experience as a teacher-educator, I have observed that it takes about three years of practice, supported by staff development and peer critique, to enable teachers to develop the new skills and knowledge they need to effectively use media texts in the classroom to promote critical-thinking and analysis skills'.

According to Powers (2010, pp. 37) though, education schools that prepare today's teachers do not offer instruction on how to incorporate news literacy instruction into the classroom or test teachers on this content area. One possible explanation for such barriers to bringing news literacy into the classroom are arguably systemic, rooted in society's fundamental perceptions and attitudes towards the news media.

For example, Altschull (1990, pp. 53) suggests that news literacy has consistently been viewed as a discipline of practice, 'not one of deep and reflective thought'. Similarly, Hobbs (2004, pp. 51) writes,

'Although the use of popular-culture materials is becoming more and more common, there is little widespread public enthusiasm for the use of popular mass media texts among education and business leaders, and even less among parents and community leaders'.

An obvious reason for this is that news literacy might be seen as a tool by some for propagandising by the teacher. In other words, there may be concern that news literacy lessons come with political judgments. As Powers (2010, pp. 43) writes though,

'While maintaining absolute political objectivity is impossible for teachers introducing any classroom lesson, proponents of news literacy emphasise that the instruction is about teaching skills rather than ideological values'.

Indeed, news literacy education is not about teaching students what to think when it comes to news – quite the contrary, it is about teaching students how to think critically about the news they read. Nonetheless, misconceptions about the pedagogy underlying news literacy needs to be taken into account as a widespread barrier for its inclusion into curricula.

A final factor to consider is that many classrooms may be ill-equipped with the technological resources necessary to facilitate lessons on news literacy. According to the report "The Internet and the Threat It Poses to Local Media: Lessons from News in the Schools", one-third of teachers said they are not making as much use of Internet-based news as they would like, because their classrooms are not equipped for it (Patterson, 2010, pp. 5). The necessity of computers and Internet access is particularly apparent when one refers to global news literacy, in which the reading of news from international outlets online would be a prerequisite. As some schools lack computers, wireless access, or the projection technology necessary for teachers to effectively draw on digital news as an educational resource, this problem is an immediate barrier to the inclusion of news literacy lessons. That being said, there are approaches that teachers can take to respond to such technological obstacles, which might include rationing students' access to equipment or applying a "bring your own device" (BYOD) policy in the classroom. Such approaches to overcoming technological resource constraints are not necessarily ideal and may present their own problems. As a result, the inclusion of news literacy curricula needs to be considered on a case-by-case basis, specifically taking account of the school's access to relevant technologies.

Given all of the barriers to news literacy education in schools, its advocates face an important task ahead. Hobbs (2010, pp. 8) suggests greater efforts needs to be made to help educators see the value of employing news and current events into K-12 and higher education. Powers (2010, pp. 45) writes recognition is needed 'that news literacy involves critical thinking skills, a commonly listed learning objective, and that acquiring the ability to critically analyse news and public affairs information promotes good citizenship'. In this way, it is much more likely that news literacy education will be represented in educational standards, which reflect the policy consensus of what teachers are expected to cover and what students are expected to learn.

Case-studies of News Literacy in the Classroom

The Powerful Voices for Kids Program

This was a university-school partnership program, which involved Temple University students working with small groups of children (ages 9 to 11) to develop their news literacy skills during July 2010. The young age of the participants makes this program particularly unique. According to Powers (2010, pp. 2) targeting middle and high school students is wise though, because these are the years when many people begin developing their reading and viewing routines. The younger news literacy can be taught therefore, the better. Hobbs (2010) observed this program closely, reporting it to be a perfect example of "what works" in news literacy education, and she uses this to draw fundamental learning principles that should guide the pedagogy of news literacy.

Hobbs focuses specifically on one group of children who were involved in a project where they explored just one news story in depth: the violence associated with flash mobs in Philadelphia. Using the simple programming tool, Scratch, the children made interactive media about the news event, which stimulated conversation about how the news is constructed and why news is so important in society. Hobbs (2010) reveals key learning outcomes of this project for the children, which made them more aware of the role of news in society, how to assess its reliability and the impact news can have on others.

Commenting on the learning outcomes of the program, McManus (2009) states that:

'In my view, these are the kinds of insights that are now essential for people to be full participants in contemporary society. These are habits of mind that will enable young people to flourish in the tsunami of information that surrounds them, where news pretenders offer "fake news" and where cheapening and corner-cutting interfere in cash-strapped news organisations leads to a diminution of quality news and information'.

According to Hobbs (pp. 4), the success of the program was achieved by building critical thinking and communication skills. In contrast to the transmission model of education, the program begins from the learner's interests: 'Learners, not teachers select the topic to examine, and they select news that's personally meaningful to them'. In the teaching process, students are also encouraged to ask critical questions, using reasoning and evidence to support their ideas. This method is particularly appropriate for the area that Hobbs refers to as 'constructedness', in which careful attention is paid to how news stories are constructed.

News Literacy Program at Stony Brook University

Fleming (2013) provides a case study that focuses on one of the most ambitious and well-funded curricular news literacy programs. Ideologically, the News Literacy Program at Stony Brook is similar to the Powerful Voices for Kids Program, but it is an ongoing program that exclusively involves university students. Fleming describes it as an experiment in modern journalism education and media literacy. This is because traditionally, journalism has had a practice-oriented philosophy, and yet as Fleming (pp. 2) explains, the program at Stony Brook 'veered off of journalism education's skills-development tradition and into unchartered territory called news literacy'. Howard Schneider, the founding dean of the School of Journalism at Stony Brook University, designed the program with the objective that young audiences would sharpen their critical thinking skills and come to support high-quality news. According to Fleming (2013, pp. 11), Schneider feared that important news literacy principles of the press were disappearing as the lines of "responsible" journalism and 'everything else blurred in the fast-moving digital sea of information and disinformation'.

The approach at Stony Brook is in line with suggestions made by Mihailidis that news literacy programs should not just focus on critiquing news content, but should also focus on understanding and contextualising it. According to Fleming (2013, pp. 13), this translates into an instructional strategy that teaches students how to access, evaluate, analyse, and appreciate journalism. As with the Powerful Voices for Kids Program, the success of news literacy education then is largely derived from creating what Hobbs (1998, pp. 28) calls a 'pedagogy of inquiry', "asking critical questions about what you watch, see, and read". The ultimate objective is to promote critical thinking skills, which develop intellectual autonomy on the part of the student. The broader goal of critical thinking, according to Mihailidis (2011, pp. 4), guards against taking the mediated environment for granted. After all, as media scholar Marshall McLuhan (1969, pp. 5) pointed out, humans live in constructed media environments as unconsciously as fish live in water.

News literacy education must therefore help students understand and analyse the constructions of reality presented by journalists, which sometimes offer incomplete or inaccurate portrayals of the world we live in. This would explain the overall objectives of both the Powerful Voices for Kids Program and the news literacy course at Stony Brook, which is for students to become more regular and more sceptical news readers, who are able to accurately assess the reliability of the news. Fleming (2013, pp. 13) presents results that instructional approaches based on this approach to news literacy, include high levels of engagement, a greater awareness of current events, and deeper, more nuanced understandings of journalism.

The Stony Brook program has been criticised for not giving any attention to ownership issues. Kellner and Share (2007, pp. 61) for example, state that instruction on how ownership influences news judgment and perpetuates oppressive depictions of race, class, and gender in news content is of utmost importance to critical media literacy educators. Likewise,

Ashley et al. (2010, pp. 37) suggests that it would be helpful for news consumers to know who owns the media companies that produce the news, since this can shape the content of the news. The incentive to maximise profit may limit the diversity of views presented for instance, and this can be seen as a disservice to democracy, which is dependent on a free and independent press. However, Fleming (2013, pp. 13) plays down the importance of this, suggesting that the approach to news literacy instruction at Stony Brook need not conform to what she calls 'critical media literacy principles' at a time when 'the power of a select few profit-seeking news organisations dominating the public agenda is eroding as news audiences increasingly scatter across social and other media to satisfy their information needs'.

Moreover, as alluded to by Mihailidis (2011, pp. 28), the goal of news literacy should not simply be to generate distrust or cynicism about the news because otherwise, news literacy programs might lead to dismissive attitudes about the press and civic responsibilities in general. In one of his studies for example, Mihailidis (pp. 30) finds that a class focused on news was successful in developing critical reading and viewing skills, but it also seemed to encourage cynical views of the press. A balance needs to be struck therefore, between teaching critical thinking skills and at the same time fostering appropriate personal interpretation habits about the news. It is this approach that seems to be exemplified by both the Powerful Voices for Kids Program and the Stony Brook news literacy program, which equips students to demand and appreciate quality journalism that adheres to the norms to which it aspires.

Aside from their effective pedagogies, the success of these two programs can be attributed to the ready availability of appropriate technologies and access to diverse news sources. These two factors both facilitate the fundamental objectives of news literacy, but unfortunately also represent the key challenges in the programs' replication. Fleming (2013, pp. 14) for example, states that the Stony Brook approach is not without fault because 'of its cost, dependence on PowerPoint presentations, and last-minute updates'. Similarly, the Powerful Voices for Kids Program relies on the distribution of age-appropriate news articles, coding software (Scratch) and the support of university students. Discussing information obesity, Whitworth (2009, pp. 2) states that:

'At the very least, we will suffer a loss in quality of engagement, and require new tools and strategies to deal with the overload'.

176

This same statement can be applied equally well to the challenges facing news consumers. Both the Powerful Voices for Kids and Stony Brook Program clearly have appropriate strategies in place to deal with the large quantity of news online, helping students to navigate and analyse this information.

30. Key points from Part Three

- Bloom's taxonomy is a powerful tool, which can be used to underpin planning, shape activities and inform questioning. By using keywords and question stems aligned with the different levels of the taxonomy, it becomes possible to challenge students' thinking and raise achievement.

- When successful teaching is taking place, learning is visible.

- Teachers should collaborate with other teachers, to discuss their teaching.

- One of the things all successful teachers do is to make their lessons meaningful, for example, through the use of stories.

- Feedback is an incredibly powerful influence on student achievement.

- Effective feedback is impossible without first having effective assessment strategies in place.

- Digital portfolios are particularly useful for formative assessment because they can serve as an administrative tool to manage and organise students' work.

- Initiatives such as Flipped Learning and Genius Hour can be seen to encourage students' creativity and motivation, while paving the way for them to become lifelong learners.

- Given the immense potential for learning opportunities to be made possible by smartphones and other Internet-connected devices, it is only logical to harness and leverage this technology in order to enrich students' learning.

- News literacy has become increasingly important area of digital citizenship that ought to be taught.

- The News Literacy Project website https://newslit.org/educators/sift/ provides a useful online tool for teachers and students, to improve their news literacy skills.

PART FOUR

Educational Resources

Technology is just a tool. In terms of getting the kids working together and motivating them, the teacher is most important.

– Bill Gates

31. Appropriate Technology for Education

Digital technology over recent years has had an enormous impact on education. Representing the second main wave of disruptive technology since the printing press, digital technology, namely computers and the Internet, have fundamentally changed how students learn and teachers teach. As we have touched upon already, education is much more accessible now, and teachers have the tools to communicate more engagingly than ever before. To go forward from here then, one should consider both when and how to use technology for the classroom, to best support teaching and learning.

Education and technology are strongly related. This is demonstrated by the many technologies, old and new, that are used in classrooms everyday by teachers and students alike. In her book, *Teaching as a Design Science*, Diana Laurillard (2012) makes the interesting observation that education does not drive technological invention. Instead, education tends to be beholden to the inventiveness of other fields such as business and leisure. There are now a wide array of different "educational" technologies available (laptops, iPads, projectors, etc.), yet very few have their origins specifically within the classroom context.

Appropriate technology in an educational setting should therefore be assessed for its potential to meet educational aims. In the chapters that follow, we will look closely at different technologies that can be used in the classroom. The full potential of these educational technologies though, is only realised when they support creativity and critical thinking. In order to better understand how to evaluate the appropriateness of educational technology, it is important to identify what educational aims are, what educational technology is and how **appropriate** educational technology should be defined.

The current definition of educational technology from the Association for Education Communications & Technology (AECT) is as follows: *Educational technology is the study and ethical practice of facilitating learning and improving performance by creating, using, and managing appropriate technological processes and resources.* The sheer breadth of what form technology can take and how it interacts with the learning environment has important implications for its potential to 'facilitate learning and improve performance.' For instance, both a pencil and a laptop can be seen as different types of technologies for use in the classroom. However, this does not mean that either tool is necessarily appropriate for all classrooms or lessons all of the time. What facilitates learning for one context or situation does not necessarily do so for all.

Traditionally, the concept of appropriate technology has been discussed with respect to economic development. The British economist, Schumacher was the first to formerly posit the notion. The criteria for appropriate technology is encapsulated in his book, Small Is Beautiful (1973), in which he states that it should be: (a) simple, (b) small scale, (c) low cost, and (d) non-violent. Although the definition has subsequently been adapted by others, from the educational perspective, it suffices to stick with the original criteria. The rationale underpinning the criteria is that 'new possibilities are created for people, singly or collectively, to help themselves' (1980, pp. 57). This certainly ties into what most educators are trying to do, which is to develop independent learners. Irrespective of context or situation, classroom or lesson, the core idea presented by Schumacher is that when it comes to the aim of empowering people by use of appropriate technology, less is *more*. From a pedagogical standpoint, appropriate technology would imply itself to be easily and non-invasively assimilated into the learning environment of the classroom.

The appropriateness of technology according to Schumacher's criteria is positively related to the degree of what Mishra & Koelher (2006) have referred to as "transparency", i.e. the extent to which the technology blends into the environment such that it is not even considered a technology anymore. These technologies, which have become so commonplace such as pens and exercise books, are now rendered as "transparent". Arguably, this is in contrast to digital technologies for example, which are not as deeply assimilated into the educational system and therefore not as "transparent". Diana Laurillard (2012, pp. 210) supports such an assertion: 'the story of digital learning technologies has hardly begun, and there will be no end until they have become so fully embedded in education that we will not even ask the question….(Paper) is now so completely embedded, and it is so diverse in its benefits, that no-one begins to ask how "effective" it is.' A "transparent" technology then can certainly be seen to meet Schumacher's criteria.

The greater the transparency (and therefore appropriateness) of educational

180

technology, the greater its effectiveness insofar as facilitating teaching and learning.

Transparency alone, although for the most part a necessary condition, is not a sufficient condition in determining the appropriateness of technology in the classroom setting. Rosemary Luckin (2006) discusses teaching and learning as taking place within an 'ecology' – a dynamic and constantly-evolving interaction between a wide range of resources. She refers to this dynamic as 'The Learner Centric Ecology of Resources Model' and argues that such a model helps us to design educational experiences that are relevant to the learner's needs. Ultimately, this model sets the context in which technologies are used and in part, determines the appropriateness of their use. Most importantly, it shows us that a technology appropriate for one classroom is not necessarily appropriate for another. This is because the model is made up of resources, which include knowledge on the part of the teacher and learner. In the case of interactive whiteboards for example, some teachers are very knowledgeable in how to effectively use this technology, whereas others are not. To this extent, it can be seen that the appropriateness of technology is defined by the user. Punya Mishra and Matthew Koelher (2006) refer to a very specific type of knowledge that the teacher needs: Technological Pedagogical Content Knowledge (TPCK), arguing that this complex type of knowledge is required for thoughtful pedagogical uses of technology. As the technology is used more regularly and becomes embedded in the classroom, its "transparency" not only increases to better facilitate the pedagogy, but the technology itself is also used more effectively by the class teacher as the teacher's TPCK improves.

The relatively recent arrival of digital technologies is still filtering its way down into the educational system. Education will have to adapt in order to be able to fully embrace digital technology. Indeed, most schools are now only just starting to fully integrate digital applications into their ICT curriculums, much less the curriculum as a whole and are therefore not adequately preparing students for ICTs in real world contexts. Prior to the overhaul in the English ICT curriculum (now called 'Computing'), the former UK Education Secretary, Michael Gove had branded the ICT curriculum in England's schools as a 'mess'. Until recently, a lot of ICT education had been inappropriate for today's needs. Much more emphasis in particular is now needed on teaching students to use open source software from an earlier age, as the core principles of open source are being recognised by the wider community.

What sets open source software apart from other technologies is that it is much more people centred than closed source software. As Pearce (2012) points out, 'Where Microsoft might utilise a few thousand programmers and software engineers to debug their code, the Linux community has access to hundreds of thousands of programmers debugging, rewriting, and submitting code.' It is this type of mass-scale collaboration that is driving the success of other Web 2.0 applications such as social networking sites and wikis. In education, moves have been made in this direction with the high-profile case of Nicholas Negroponte's "One Laptop Per Child" project, which fully embraces open source software. By bringing about greater connectivity by means of collaboration such projects serve as a vehicle to empower teachers and students, particularly in the developing world where lack of access to key information can be a critical issue. This can also help to bridge the so-called digital divide in which there is a gap between different groups of people in terms of their effective access to digital and information technology.

Pearce uses Appropedia as an example of an 'Open source appropriate technology' website, where a large number of participants are allowed to create and modify the content directly from their web browsers. Education has slowly followed suit with similar open source resources such as 'Curriki' and 'Connexions', which facilitate collaboration and access to free instructional materials for educators. The appropriateness of such sites are measured insofar as they 'simplify the administration of collaboratively organising information, project examples, best practices, and "how tos"' (Pearce et al. 2010). In so doing, open source software can be the solution to the problem of access to critical information for sustainable development.

Clearly, any medium that enhances peer communication is a step in the right direction towards achieving greater levels of appropriateness. Early in my own teaching practice for example, I organised blogs for all students in the latter years of their primary education. The purpose of these blogs was to digitalise paper-based book reviews that the children had to do in the past. It represented a cheaper and simpler alternative to photocopying and distributing copious paper book review templates. By encouraging greater collaboration and increasing the accountability of both the student and class teacher, these blogs helped to improve the quality of students' written work, as they are effectively publishing it for the whole school community to see. In the process, the children learnt important digital literacies, such as netiquette and how best to search for information online. It also served for a smoother transition into secondary school, where secondary students are having to setup and manage their own wiki spaces. In these ways, the use of blogs represents an appropriate use of digital technology for educational purposes.

Appropriate technology can take the form of many different tools. As

182

technology becomes more "transparent" to the extent that it is embedded in the classroom, it more closely aligns itself with Schumacher's criterion. In addition, the extent to which a technology empowers students to become more independent learners and teachers to deliver more engaging lessons should be seen to be at the heart of determining the appropriateness of educational technologies because this is what education is all about. However, the extent that educational technologies achieves these aims is largely contingent upon TPCK, as teachers need specific pedagogical and content knowledge to use technology thoughtfully.

Moreover, the emergence of Web 2.0 applications and specifically open source software models, identify the need for appropriate technology to be people-centred. This is because the more people developing the software, the more the software is going to benefit from being of better quality and greater reliability. Independent of the technology though, as educators we need to make sure that it is of greatest benefit to teaching and learning. This can only be achieved by embedding the technology into our daily pedagogy such that it is not out of place and can be used very naturally by teachers and learners alike.

32. Digital Learning Platforms

Out of all the digital learning platforms I have had experience of using, with children from 5 to 14 years, one of the best is BrainPOP. The site has a library of hundreds of videos, which are all searchable by topic. The videos are generally no more than five-minutes long, and using the two main animated characters, Tim & Moby, BrainPOP simplifies topics for children, making them engaging, fun and easy to follow.

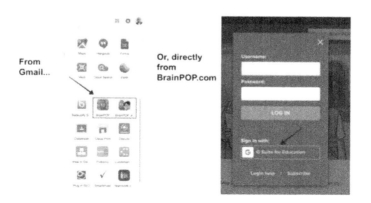

BrainPOP can be accessed from either Google Apps for Education (if integrated with Google Apps for Education) or from the site, Brainpop.com.

At the conclusion of the video, students have the option to complete a variety of follow-up activities:

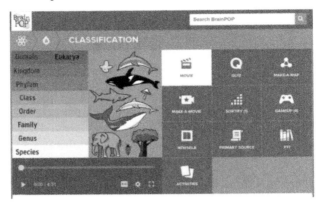

Activities include quizzes, interactive games, sorting tasks, concept map creation, vocabulary review, and news article analysis, among others.

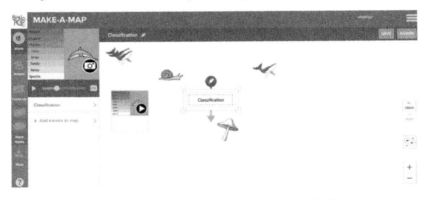

The mind mapping software is very easy to use. It contains a stock of images to use as well as the functionality to take freeze frames of the BrainPOP animation, to use as images.

Species definitions are very different for dolphins, humans

New species of insects, worms and other creepy-crawlers are announced on a basis. Similarly, just last week, two new humpback dolphin species splashed i headlines, while in October, news broke that early humans may have include species than previously thought. This raises the question: what does it take to distinct species?

More than 70 official species definitions exist, of which 48 are widely accepted, by scientists. There's no hard rule that scientists must use only one definition. Some apply a handful of species definitions when approaching the topic.

"I personally go to my lab every day and use five species definitions to conduct research," says Sergios-Orestis Kolokotronis, a molecular ecologist at Fordham University, and co-author of the new dolphin study, published in Molecular Ecology. "And I sleep just fine amidst this uncertainty."

Species definitions do not always translate from one organism to another. Dolphins may become isolated by distance and behavior that prevents them from reproducing, but in other cases, these distinguishing markers distance and behavior do not apply. For

One of my favourite resources from BrainPOP is Newsela, which provides a different comprehension text for each topic available on the site. What is particularly useful about Newsela is the functionality to change the word count of the text, which can make the text simpler or more complex depending on the reader – great for differentiation!

As BrainPOP integrates with Google Apps Suite for Education, all of these activities have built-in functionality that allow students to submit responses to their teacher. This submission may come in the form of a quiz response, student-created concept map or completed vocabulary worksheet, for example. Students can then track their submissions, grades, and feedback by navigating to their My BrainPop page. Teachers have additional access to the BrainPop Educators page, which is included as a link with each video and offers user-submitted and BrainPop-created lesson plans, printables, and instructional resources.

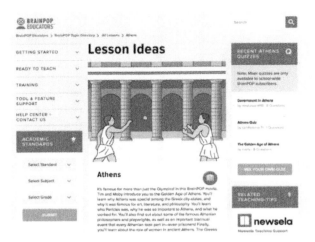

BrainPop also enables teachers to create and assign their own quizzes for a given topic. They can write their own multiple choice or open-ended quiz questions, or they can opt to pull items from BrainPop's library of over several thousand questions.

Some of the content can be relatively high level for primary children, as the site is designed for students from 8 to 14 years. This why there is a sister site, BrainPop Junior (included within the subscription package), which has been designed for children from 5 to 8 years. In addition, there is BrainPop ELL for new English language learners.

Teachers manage their classes and access all submitted student work via the My BrainPop page. From here teachers see a history of all student submissions and are able to review, grade, and provide feedback to students.

I designed the website, Classroom Flipped (http://classroomflipped.com/) to provide access to BrainPOP topics that match our International Primary Curriculum (IPC). The name, Classroom Flipped, actually comes from the educational approach known as flipped learning, which was discussed earlier. The website includes a section specifically for STEAM, with links to the best resources on the Web, including relevant high quality, age-appropriate educational videos, games, articles and interactive quizzes.

As a tool for Flipped Learning, BrainPOP has many benefits. Students can research plenty of child-friendly resources using this platform. It can save teachers lots of time searching for appropriate videos and enables them to spend more time as facilitators of learning. The platform is also compatible with mobile devices such as iPads and smartphones, which makes it another great application to use as part of a BYOD initiative.

33. STEAM

STEAM is both an acronym and an educational approach. As an acronym, STEAM stands for Science, Technology, Engineering, Art and Mathematics. As an educational approach, STEAM is about facilitating learning experiences across these five subject areas.

Since the late 1990s there has been an increasing global focus on the need to better prepare students for the 21st century workforce by equipping them with the skills and knowledge in STEAM subjects. After all, the most in-demand jobs globally fall into one or more of these five subject areas.

According to the Rhode Island School of Design, which adds the arts to the original STEM framework, *"The goal (of STEAM) is to foster the true innovation that comes with combining the mind of a scientist or technologist with that of an artist or designer."* All technology begins and ends with some form of art. In fact, the arts and sciences are a natural match when students have sufficient time for project development, reflection and revision. For example, arts are used in website and user interface design, advertising and the design of literally any product imaginable.

Many schools around the world, my own included, have made inroads in teaching STEAM through various initiatives, including (but not limited to):

- using Computing & ICT to permeate across the whole school curriculum, thereby linking these five disciplines

- after-school makerspace clubs or program

- holistic, thematic curricula such as the IPC or PYP, where projects using STEAM practices are embedded

- BYOD initiatives (bring your own device)

- staff training to encourage hands-on exploration within each of these disciplines

- robotics programs

The STEAM approach is intended to be holistic, bringing these five disciplines together.

An integral part of learning STEAM should be about making and tinkering. As educators, we are always looking for ways to inspire creativity and wonder in our students. The sort of projects made possible by STEAM can create classrooms of joy, revolution and invention. Making and tinkering are powerful forms of learning by doing, an ethos shared by the maker community and many educators.

STEAM is not just about using digital technologies though; STEAM activities can be as simple as just using a piece of paper. For example, below is one of the activities we gave our staff was to do when introducing

188

what STEAM is all about:

STEAM Challenge

- Build the highest possible tower you can that holds a book at least 16 cm above the ground for a minimum of 3 seconds (the book must rest on top of the tower)
- The tower must be free-standing, which means no taping or holding to the floor.

Time: 20 minutes (including testing)

Materials: 10 sheets of newspaper and 50 cm of tape,

Group Size: Maximum of 4 people

Success Criteria – The tallest tower wins as long as...

- Tower is free-standing

- Tower is able to hold the weight of a book for a minimum of 3 seconds

- Book must be resting a minimum of 16cm above the ground

- Tower is constructed solely of newspaper and masking tape

This challenge was a great example of the collaboration, creativity and enquiry-based learning that STEAM activities can promote.

All our staff managed to build a free-standing paper tower, but to ensure that it was taller than 16cm was not easy!

For more activities and ideas related to STEAM, you can take a look at my STEAM page here (http://classroomflipped.com/steam.php).

34. Makerspaces & Digital Technologies

A makerspace is a unique, multipurpose learning environment that encourages tinkering, play and open-ended exploration. Such activities demand an enquiry-based approach to learning, and they epitomise what progressive education is all about. The central idea of a makerspace is that children learn by doing.

The only thing that is required of such an initiative is a room with appropriate materials and resources, to encourage learners to make. It also serves as a central location, where all of these resources can both be stored

190

and used.

Although having a makerspace initiative can fit in very well a school's commitment to STEAM (Science, Technology, Engineering & Maths) education, it is worth pointing out that our makerspace is not just for STEAM classes. Video production, for example, forms a big part of what the room can be used for, and this goes hand in hand with other subjects like literacy and drama. In this way, making can be anything to anyone!

Pedagogically, the whole maker movement is underpinned by the idea of "constructionism", which was a term first coined by the American educator and writer, Seymour Papert. It is a similar-sounding term to the more well-known pedagogy, constructivism. Where constructivism is a well-established theory of learning indicating that people actively construct new knowledge by combining their experiences with what they already know, constructionism takes things a step further. Although the learning happens inside the learner's head, Papert's constructionism states that this happens most reliably when the learner is engaged in a personally meaningful activity outside of their head that makes the learning real and shareable.

In other words, when students are consciously engaged in making things for others, learning happens most effectively. The collaborative and sharing functionality of the web certainly makes this very easy. Students can now use software like Scratch or Google Apps for Education for example, to create their own programs and digital content, and then share this with the rest of the world. This interaction made possible is probably the greatest benefit of the Web for educational use. This is exciting because it increases

191

the potential for students to achieve greater levels of success than would otherwise be the case.

According to Sylvia Martinez and Gary Stager (2013), authors of *Invent to Learn*:

'This shareable activity may take the form of a robot, musical composition, poem, conversation, or new hypothesis... This is much more than "hands-on" learning. The meaningful part of constructionism is not just touchy-feely new age language. It acknowledges that the power of making something comes from a question or an impulse that the learner has, and is not imposed from the outside... We seek to liberate learners from their dependency on being taught.'

By creating a makerspace, students are given the opportunity to take ownership of their own learning as they explore their own passions. Nevertheless, it is still possible to teach basic skills, and then "flip" the makerspace, so that students can innovate and build on what they have learnt.

A makerspace is a fantastic way to bring creativity into the students' learning and support deeper learning - adding value to what we already do. Makerspaces can be the perfect environments in which to challenge students, to try to solve problems in new ways. These challenges can be created by either teachers or students. What is particularly exciting about the makerspace concept, is how this can impact lessons, as teachers can become more innovative owing to the various tools easily accessible.

Simon Sinek's book, *Start With Why*, talks about the importance of knowing your *why*: the purpose, cause or belief that inspires you to do what you do. This is as important to keep in mind when designing a makerspace as just about any other venture. For this reason, at the planning stage for this project, our digital leaders began by writing down the core values that our makerspace should have, and in the end, after much discussion, they settled on:

Work, Learn & Create

According to Laura Fleming, author of *The Kickstart Guide to Making Great Makerspaces*, great makerspaces begin with a vision for driving their space. As with all great ventures therefore, the next step was for the digital leaders to come up with a mission statement. In the end, we decided to borrow this slogan, which is also used by robotics construction set, littleBits:

"Make something that does something."

Regardless of the activity itself, this slogan has come to be the expectation for all our students who use the makerspace room, to make something that does something.

You can take a virtual tour of the makerspace that we created as well as find additional ideas for your own makerspace here (http://classroomflipped.com/makerspace.php).

35. iPads to Enhance Learning

In this chapter, I discuss some examples of specific iPad apps, to enhance teaching and learning. My experience with using iPads in the classroom has been positive. They can be introduced relatively seamlessly into most lessons across the curriculum, and there are so many apps to choose from, that you are sure to find one to suit the needs of you or your students. I have put together the list below of my all-time favourite apps for use both at home and at school.

Most of these apps are for use with younger children (less than 10 years old):

Book Creator - this is a brilliant app for supporting children in creating their own multimedia books, as it enables them to easily combine text, images and sounds.

Comic Life – provides a fun way for children to create comic strips using traditional templates. Photographs can be inserted with various call outs, text boxes and speech bubbles.

iCardSort – more for use at home than at school, this app provides digital sticky notes, which can help older learners to organise their ideas and revise learning.

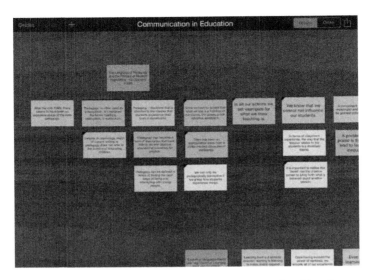

The iPad App, iCardSort can be used to quickly summarise key ideas from any text.

<u>Even Monsters Get Sick</u> – this is a really engaging interactive story for young children. They learn the basics of how to treat people who are unwell while improving their reading skills.

<u>iWriteWords</u> – one for younger children, this app helps with letter pronunciation, basic spellings and handwriting. Easy and fun to use, this app quickly engages children.

<u>iMovie</u> – I have used this app a lot with students of all ages to make educational videos. It is easy to learn and allows you to create your own video projects on the fly from scratch or create a movie trailer using a template.

<u>Math Vs Zombies</u> - in this app children have to quickly answer maths questions to defeat zombies before they can attack. The game progresses through a number of levels and includes addition, subtraction and multiplication questions.

<u>PDF Expert</u> – makes it easy to annotate, organise and view documents as PDFs.

<u>Percy Parker</u> – this app sets each of the times-tables to catchy music and is a great way to engage children with learning their times-tables.

<u>Planet Geo</u> – this app is brilliant for developing young children's geographical knowledge, as it teaches them to identify different countries,

194

cities, flags and World Heritage Sites.

Puppet Pals HD – children I have taught have loved this app. It encourages children to develop their speaking and storytelling skills through the use of digital puppets. It is also an app that can be used by teachers to create child friendly video content.

SpellBoard – helps children to learn their weekly spellings. All you need to do is enter the spellings and the app will generate customisable tests for you, which then stores a record of children's progress. You can also add pictures to the words as well as record words and sentences using your own voice.

Stop Motion – children can create stop motion animated movies quickly using this app. It is simple to use, as you can copy, paste, delete and insert frames at any position.

WordFoto – this app allows you to take a photograph and then add ten words, which are wrapped and morphed against the picture. It is a simple idea, which can be used for descriptive writing and poetry.

In this example, I just chose a photo from my camera roll and wrote four words: 'Learners', 'Digital', 'Create' and 'Technology'. In less than a second, the WordFoto app converts my picture into artwork made up of the words I have chosen. There is a limit of ten words per picture and shorter words generally look better. The quality of the new image created depends on the quality of the original.

Video production using the Padcaster & green screen

One of the main uses of iPads can be to record and edit video. The Ultimate Studio kit includes a tripod, green screen, wide lens (that connects to the front of the iPad), teleprompter, three different microphones and a lighting system.

Padcaster & Green Screen

Students can use the Padcaster and green screen technology for example, to create their own persuasion adverts. Green screen technology is used all

196

the time to enhance digital creations in the movies and on TV. For instance, a green screen can make it look like actors are driving across the dessert, or a news announcer is standing in front of an animated weather map. By inserting an iPad into the aluminum and rubber casing of the Padcaster, students can record high quality video. Along with the app, Do Ink, students are able to create the illusion of many different backdrops to make their persuasive arguments even more compelling!

The combination of the Do Ink app and the Padcaster makes it easy for students to create high quality green screen videos. Featured in "Best New Apps in Education", the Do Ink app lets you combine photos and videos from the camera roll with live video from the iPad's camera. The final results have been excellent, opening possibilities for its use across the school curriculum.

Augmented Reality

Augmented Reality (AR) is a type of virtual reality that blends the real scene viewed by the user with a virtual scene generated by the computer. This composite view is designed to enhance the user's sensory perception of the real world they are seeing or interacting with.

The technology, as most of us know it today, is still in its infancy. The explosion in the popularity of smartphones and other touch screen devices though, has led to the creation of various augmented reality applications. When most people first interact with augmented reality, they

197

are amazed at what the technology can do. By layering data and information on top of the real world, augmented reality presents some exciting possibilities for the classroom, as it can help to increase student engagement and understanding of a lesson.

Below I list the best AR apps that I have discovered for use in the classroom:

1. HP Reveal allows people to turn everyday objects and images into an interactive opportunity. Using an iPad for example, you simply take a photo of an object, and then choose one of the many animations or images (or photos/videos that you have taken yourself) to overlay on top of the object. Whenever you then scan the object using the HP Reveal app, the object's image triggers the augmented reality – whichever animation you have chosen suddenly becomes visible.

In this example, this box of English tea bags triggers the HP Reveal app to produce a video of the British National Anthem.

There are many ways HP Reveal could be used in the classroom. For example, teachers could create an interactive word wall – for every word on display, a relevant photo or video could be triggered by the HP Reveal app, which helps students to remember the words. Another possibility is to create an interactive newspaper article – just like in the Harry Potter films, the photo in the article could be programmed to turn into a video.

2. CyberChase Shape Quest - This app is aimed at children ages 6 to 9, helping them to use their geometry and spatial reasoning to develop problem solving skills. Once the app is installed, you just need a printout of the game board. The children can then hover the iPad over the game board to trigger the augmented reality gaming experience. Unlike other games out there, this gets the children moving their whole bodies around the game board in order to interact with the game.

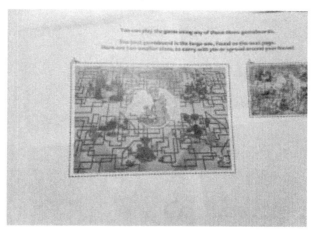

The printouts of the game board come in three different sizes – small, medium and large. These can then be handed out to students, who will then be able to use the Space Quest app to scan the game board and play.

The game makes full use of augmented reality, getting the user to complete tasks by manoeuvring the iPad around the game board.

3. Spacecraft 3D – A great app to accompany any topic on space, Spacecraft 3D enables you to find out about the variety of spacecraft that are used to explore our solar system. Using printed AR images and the camera on the iPad, you get to see the robotic explorers close up.

Spacecraft 3D provides extremely realistic looking 3D images of the different spacecrafts used to explore our solar system.

4. The **AR Flashcards** are great for early years. Simply print out print out the AR cards (provided as a PDF document on the developer's homepage), and you're ready to go. The developer has the following apps available that are well worth using with younger children:

- *AR Flashcards Animal Alphabet* – with this app, you get 26 augmented reality animals, one for each letter. The app also includes dinosaur cards to help you learn the names of some of the different dinosaurs.

This is a great app for teaching young children about the letters of the alphabet. The 3D images wobble slightly as well, giving them a natural feel.

- *AR Flashcards Space* – this app includes 10 augmented reality planets to help you learn the solar system. By tapping on each planet, you can hear its name, and tapping on the info button provides an interesting fact.

An ideal app for learning about the different planets in the solar system, AR Flashcards Space could be used with students of any age.

- *AR Flashcards Shapes & Colors* – this is a basic app to learn the names of the 3D shapes. As with the other apps in the AR Flashcards series, you can interact with the objects by tapping on the screen. This app has a colour bar at the top of the screen that will actively change the shape's colour, helping children to learn the colour names as well.

This is a really creative app and one of my favourites. It makes use of a circus theme, as each 3D figure is holding or balancing on a different shape. I think this is an enchanting way for young children to learn the names of shapes and colours.

5. Quiver is a brilliant app for all ages, but can be especially useful for younger children. Making use of a variety of colouring pages, which are available from the Quiver website for all subject areas, the colouring pages become 3D on your iPad just as you have coloured them!

The first step is to colour the colouring page. Whichever page you pick, it will need to be downloaded onto the iPad beforehand in order for the augmented reality to work. This only needs to be done once, and then it will work straightaway.

Hovering the iPad over your coloured image will activate the augmented reality, displaying a 3D version of your coloured image.

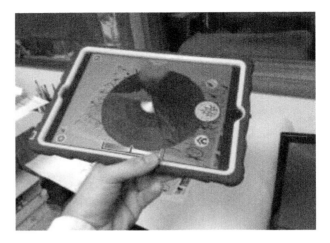

Each colouring page has its own animated actions that the user can interact with.

Teachers are still pioneering how augmented reality can best be used in the classroom. One thing is for sure though, that with the right apps, students' engagement and overall level of understanding can be increased. By providing a completely different interface in which to interact with the environment around us, there are many possibilities for how AR technology can be used in the classroom and developed in the future. The apps discussed in this chapter provide a good place to start.

36. Key points from Part Four

- One should consider both when and how to use technology for the classroom, to best support teaching and learning.

- The appropriateness of technology is positively related to its "transparency", i.e. the extent to which the technology blends into the environment such that it is not even considered a technology anymore.

- Pedagogically speaking, the greater the transparency (and therefore appropriateness) of educational technology, the greater its effectiveness insofar as facilitating teaching and learning.

- Teachers should also have a sound working knowledge of the technology they wish to use in order to make best use of it for teaching and learning.

- Online learning platforms such as BrainPOP provide many

excellent videos and quizzes, which are all searchable by topic.

-   STEAM is both an acronym and an educational approach. As an acronym, STEAM stands for Science, Technology, Engineering, Art and Mathematics. As an educational approach, STEAM is about facilitating learning experiences across these five subject areas.

-   A makerspace is a unique, multipurpose learning environment that encourages tinkering, play and open-ended exploration.

-   By creating a makerspace, students are given the opportunity to take ownership of their own learning as they explore their own passions.

CONCLUSION

The practice that we call teaching has been in existence in one form or another since the beginning of our species. In order to meet even basic wants and needs, human beings have always passed on knowledge and skills from one individual to the next. This is what has enabled communities to grow and civilizations to develop. An individual who has an idea for example, has only an idea of limited value; knowing how to teach ideas, to share knowledge and skills has, without exception, been the key to elevating our human condition.

As human beings have been hardwired to learn in the same way for millions of years, the core principles of what constitutes successful teaching have not changed. Formal education, by contrast, is a relatively recent phenomenon – which has always been in a constant state of change, reflecting the ebb and flow of society, government priorities and school cultures.

By unpicking the many layers of what has become formal education, to the practice of teaching itself, we have seen there are three main pillars that make successful teaching possible: managing emotions, teaching strategy and educational resources. The core principles underpinning each one of these three pillars are timeless and span every context in which teaching takes place.

To be done successfully, teaching demands a great many personal qualities and professional competencies – the mastery of which, as we have seen, is a challenge. This is especially true for those new to teaching and why teacher retention continues to be an issue.

Understanding how to approach the inevitable problems associated with the teaching profession, is necessary to making its practice noble, rewarding and above all, successful. This can only be done by asking intelligent questions and digging deep into the pedagogical research to pull out hard facts and statistics about what works and what does not.

A teacher's self-regulation is critical. Beyond a teacher's subject knowledge, mastery of one's emotions ensures that a teacher can connect with and facilitate connections between other human beings. In doing so, the groundwork is set for successful behaviour management strategies, collegiality and congenial relationships with parents. Additionally, cultivating effective communication strategies and positive values such as dedication, passion and respect, are fundamentally important, ensuring that the teacher can be positive role model and an effective force in facilitating learning.

Pedagogically, successful teaching is evident when learning is visible. Among the many evidence-based teaching strategies that have proven to be successful, teachers must model and explicitly instruct students on how to learn. As well as making sure students understand the objectives and success criteria of the lesson, teachers should go through worked examples, provide opportunities for spaced practice and help students to apply key study and problem-solving skills, differentiating these strategies according to students' needs. Effective assessment strategies and quality feedback are also invaluable in terms of advancing students' learning.

Finally, teachers need appropriate tools to do their work well. The appropriateness of any particular technology can best be measured by its "transparency" – the extent to which it blends itself into the classroom environment and can quickly be adopted by teachers and students, an observation that applies to digital and non-digital tools alike. In particular, the world of digital technologies offers exciting possibilities, enabling information to be conveyed more engagingly, while facilitating greater student autonomy and opportunities for collaboration.

Although there are no simple answers, it is only through consistently practising the methods presented in this book and backed up by research, that successful teaching is made possible. We can then feel confident that all is being done to ensure our learners will flourish, putting them in good stead to live fulfilling, productive lives that make the world a better place.

INDEX

209

APPENDIX

For school trips, I provide each teacher with their own colour-coded folder, which contains everything they must know, including: staff expectations, bus groupings, room lists, maps, timetables and information about activities. On the front of their folders, I stick this 'Folder Checklist' template, to make sure they have everything:

Folder Checklist:

All staff:	✓
Staff information handout	
Orienteering activity (Petropolis Quest) x 10	
Learning activity sheets x 10	
Orienteering activity answer sheet	
Learning activity answer sheet	
Register sheet	
Student register photos	
Parent contacts	
Student medical folder (for group)* *Do not leave this on the bus - keep this with you at all times.	
Class teachers:	
Student information handouts	
SIM card storage case	
Paper clips (for removing & reinserting SIM cards)	
Mr Will, Ms Ann & Ms Lina:	
Imperial museum entrance form	
Mr Will:	
Bus signs	
Risk assessment	
Learning Activity envelopes	
Orienteering words	
School Value Certificates	
Sleeping Pizza templates	

You can also find here an exemplar handout that I wrote for staff and a similar, much shorter one, for students. By all means, as with all the resources in this book, please use and adapt this information for use on your own school trips.

(STAFF INFORMATION EXEMPLAR)

Staff Information Petrópolis Trip

Vale Real Hotel: (21) 0000-0200

Staff Expectations

- You will be responsible for ensuring the safety and good behaviour of your group.

- Remember, children's discipline is our job.

- Attend briefings in the morning at breakfast and in the evening as times may change.

- If you have any concerns or problems at any time please contact Will F.

- Be fully aware of what your group will be expected to do for each activity.

- Support the children in getting organised, but not too much!

- Looking after your group's SIM cards – distributing and ensuring collection at the appropriate time.

- Your support and active participation are required.

- Look out for children who deserve awards:

- **Compassion** - Looking after & respecting one another

- **Integrity** - Following rules & instructions

- **Determination** - Trying their best with all activities

- **Magnanimous -** Demonstrating all these three qualities

We will be awarding only one child from each subgroup an award. This can be for compassion, integrity or determination. The "Don Pedro II Magnanimous" Award, a very prestigious accolade, will go to just one child from the entire group.

Code of Conduct for Students

- Students must, at all times, follow the instructions of the Trip Leader and other supervisors.

- Students must follow the rules set by the venue of the visit.

- Students must look out for anything that might hurt them or others and tell the Trip Leader about it.

- Any equipment lost or broken on a school trip must be replaced by the student responsible.

- It is forbidden to go into other children's rooms.

- Students are not allowed to connect their mobile devices to the hotel's WiFi.

Bus Groupings

Bus 1	Bus 2	Bus 3
A1 - Ms Tracy	B2 - Ms Isabel	B1 - Ms Kelly
A2 - Mr Will	C2 - Ms Zoe	C1 - Ms Linda
	D2 - Ms Jessica	D1 - Ms Beth

(STAFF INFORMATION EXEMPLAR)

Subgroups & Room List

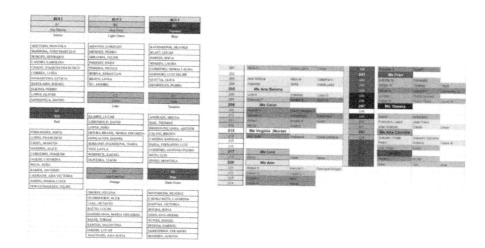

Useful Maps

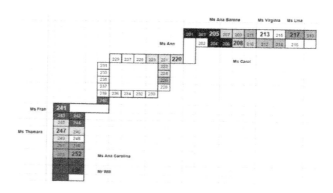

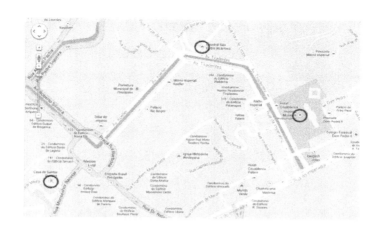

219

(STAFF INFORMATION EXEMPLAR)

Timetable – times estimated

	Morning	Afternoon and evening
Wednesday, 26th September	7:15 – Treehouse staff to arrive and to assist with organising the loading of suitcases on buses. 7:45 – All children to be in their classrooms. Register students on checklists Distribute student schedules Collect SIM cards & store in labelled wallets Instruct children to fill up their water bottle Make sure all students have gone to the bathroom 08:00 - Take children to Jubilee Hall for short briefing 08:15 - Depart for Petrópolis 10:00 - Assembly 10:30 - Fun Activity 11:30 - Lunch	12:00 - Group 1 departs for Imperial Museum 12:15 - Group 2 departs for Imperial Museum and Group 3 begins team building games 14:00 - Group 3 departs hotel for Imperial Museum 15:00 - Group 1 departs Imperial Museum for hotel 15:30 - Group 2 departs Imperial Museum for hotel 16:00 - Group 1 & 2 Team building 16:45 - Group 3 departs Imperial Museum I for hotel 17:00 - Shower & Phone calls home 18:30 - Dinner 19:45 - Hike 20:30 - Hot chocolate at hotel 21:00 - Bedtime
Thursday, 27th September	6:30 - Wake up & shower 7:00 - Breakfast 7:45 - Orienteering 09:00 - Circle time at tent area 09:30 - Snack then recreational activities 11:45 - Lunch	12:30 - Depart hotel for Santos Dumont & Cathedral 16:00 - Return to hotel 16:30 - Shower & phone calls home 18:45 - Dinner 19:30 - Disco 21:00 - Bedtime
Friday, 28th September	06:30 - Wake up & shower 07:00 - Breakfast 07:30 - Briefing in tent area 07:45 - Recreational activities 09:00 - Snack time on the balcony 10:00 - Pack bags 10:30 - Bring bags to reception 11:00 - Awards assembly 11:30 - Lunch	12:10 - Depart hotel 14:00 - Arrive at school

Learning Activities

Cathedral Digital Mural Activity - Children use camera on phone or school iPad to take and collect digital photos of interesting architectural features.

Imperial Palace - Sketch of palace & quiz questions

Santos Dumont Quest - Quiz questions

(STUDENT INFORMATION EXEMPLAR)

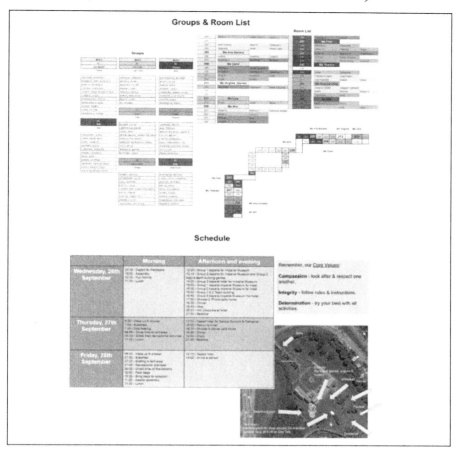

221

The following resources can be used to facilitate a Genius Hour:

Genius Hour Proposal & Planning

Student Name: _____

Teacher signature: _____

What is your Enquiry Question?

Keep in mind that the point of this project is to provide useful information, to help yourself and others understand something in-depth. Remember as well, a good enquiry question cannot immediately be answered by performing a quick Google search. This genius project requires you to get information from at least several (three or more) different places.

_____
_____

_____
_____

_____
_____

Why does this question interest you?

_____
_____

_____
_____

_____
_____

What do you wish to find out? Write a few sub-questions.

_____
_____
_____
_____
_____
_____

Where will you look to find information to answer your question?

Website:_____

Website:_____

Website:_____

Book (and author):_____

Book (and author):_____

Other:_____

What materials do you need?

_____
_____
_____
_____
_____
_____

How will you share what you have learned?

Remember, there are many ways you can present your learning. Depending on your driving question, this could be a Google Site, video, essay, Google Slide presentation, or instruction manual.

_____

_____

_____

_____

_____

_____

Genius Hour Self-Assessment Rubric

<table>
<tr>
<td></td>
<td align="center">**Highest Expectation**</td>
<td></td>
<td align="center">**Lowest Expectation**</td>
</tr>
<tr>
<td></td>
<td align="center">I couldn't have done much better.</td>
<td></td>
<td align="center">I have some improvements to make.</td>
</tr>
</table>

Effort:

5 4 3 2 1

How much time did you put in?

I spent a good amount of time outside of class reading, researching, and learning about my topic.

I mostly just glanced through stuff on the internet and maybe flipped through a book during class. I didn't spend much if any time outside of class on my project.

Inquisitiveness:

5 4 3 2 1

How motivated were you to ask questions and want answers?

I was curious and I looked up things that interested me. I'm a lifelong learner.

I didn't ask many questions just for the joy of learning, and I wasn't really interested in learning new things.

| **Originality of Ideas:** | I thought outside the box and used my imagination. | 5 4 3 2 1 | I only thought of ideas that others thought of first. I don't like new ways of doing things. I just want to stick with the old way. |
| Did you create unique ideas? | I think of ideas that others may not have. | | |

| **Overall Learning for Genius Hour Project** | Overall, I learned a lot about my topic and I don't think I could have learned much more given the time I had. | 5 4 3 2 1 | Overall, I didn't really learn much about my topic. I don't know much more than when I started my project. |

| **Overall Quality of Presentation** | My presentation was interesting and engaging for my classmates and showed how much I learned. | 5 4 3 2 1 | I didn't put enough time into my presentation. It could have been more creative and engaging. |

Briefly explain what you learned during this project.

_____

_____

226

Genius Hour Reflection

Briefly explain what you learned during this project.

_____

_____

_____

_____

_____

_____

Did what you shared with the class help (e.g. the world, your community, yourself, etc.) in some way?   Yes / No

Explain why you circled this answer:

_____

_____

_____

_____

_____

_____

For your next genius hour project, what would you do differently in terms of what you did and how you presented your project?

_____

_____

_____

_____

_____

_____

Write down 3 ideas or topics that you would like to explore for your next genius hour project:

1_____
_____

2_____
_____

3_____
_____

REFERENCES

Adams and Ovide. 2009. Newspapers Move to Outsource Foreign Coverage. The Wall Street Journal, 15 January.

Altschull, H. 1990. From Milton to McLuhan: The Ideas behind American Journalism. White Plains, NY: Longman.

Ambady, N., & Rosenthal, R. 1993. Half a minute: Predicting teacher evaluations from thin slices of nonverbal behavior and physical attractiveness. *Journal of Personality and Social Psychology, 64(3),* 431-441.

Anderson, L. W & Krathwohl, D. R., eds. 2001. A taxonomy for learning, teaching, and assessing: A revision of Bloom's taxonomy of educational objectives. Allyn and Bacon.

Anghileri, J. 1995. Children's Mathematical Thinking in the Primary Years. Cassell.

Ardley, K. 2017. 4-Day Leadership Course: Leading Learning from the Middle.

https://karenardley.com/events/leading-learning-middle-middle-leader-programme-copy/

Ashley, S, Poepsel, M, Willis, E. 2010. Media Literacy and News Credibility: Does knowledge of media ownership increase skepticism in news consumers? The National Association for Media Literacy Education's Journal of Media Literacy Education 2:1 (37 - 46)

Ashley, S, Maksl, A and Craft, S. 2013. Developing a News Media Literacy Scale. Journalism & Mass Communication Educator 68(1) 7–21

Askew, M & William, D. 1995. Recent Research in Mathematics Education 5-16. OFSTED Reviews of Research.

Atkinson, S. 1992. Mathematics with Reason. Hodder & Stoughton.

Aubrey, K and Riley, A. 2016. Understanding & Using Educational Theories. Sage Publications Ltd.

Badaracco, J. L. and Ellsworth, R. Leadership and the Quest for Integrity. Boston: Harvard Business School Press.

Beck, I., McCandliss, B.D., Sandak, R., & Perfetti, C. 2003. Focusing attention on decoding for children with poor reading skills: A study of the

Word Building intervention. Scientific Studies of Reading. 7(1),75-105.

Berger, R. 2003. An Ethic of Excellence – Building a Culture of Craftsmanship with Students. Heinemann.

Bernadowski. 2011. A Good Read: Promoting Adolescent Literacy Through Newspapers.

Blackwell, L. S., Trzesniewski, K. H. and Dweck, C. S. 2007. Implicit theories of intelligence predict achievement across an adolescent transition: A longitudinal study and an intervention. Child development, 78, 246-263, Study 1.

Bloom, B. S., Engelhart, M. D., Furst, E. J., Hill, W. H., Krathwohl, D. R. 1956. Taxonomy of educational objectives: The classification of educational goals. Handbook I: Cognitive domain. New York: David McKay Company.

Bloom, B. S. 1984. The 2 Sigma problem: The search for methods of group instruction as effective as one-to-one tutoring. Educational Researcher, 13(6), pp. 4 – 16.

Branden, N. 1994. The six pillars of self-esteem. New York.: Bantam.

Brown, J. & Staines, J. 1989. Mathematics and the Primary Curriculum. NCET.

Brown, S. & Vaughan, C. 2010. Play: How It Shapes the Brain, Opens the Imagination, and Invigorates the Soul. Penguin Putnam.

Brown, Barnfield & Stone. 1990. 'Working toward social justice' in A Spanner in the Works.

Buckingham, D. 2000. The Making of Citizens. Young People, News and Politics. Routledge.

Buckingham, D. 2003. Media Education. Literacy, Learning and Contemporary Culture. Polity Press, USA.

Burgess, D. 2012. Teach Like a Pirate. Dave Burgess Consulting Inc.

Burgoon, J. K., Berger, C. R. & Waldron, V. R. 2000. Mindfulness & interpersonal communication. Journal of Social Issues. 56(1), 105-127.

Butler, R. 1988. 'Enhancing and undermining intrinsic motivation: The effects of task-involving and ego-involving evaluation on interest and performance', British Jornal of Educational Psychology, 58(1), pp. 1-14.

230

Campione, J. C.; Brown, A. L. & Connell, M. L. 1988. Metacognition: on the importance of understanding what you are doing. In R. I. Charles & E. A. Silver (Eds.), The teaching and assessing of mathematical problem solving: pp. 93-114.

Christodoulou, D. 2013. Seven Myths About Education. The Curriculum Centre.

Clark, S. 2001. Unlocking formative assessment. London, UK: Hodder and Stoughton.

Clark, R. E. & Feldon, D. F. 2005. Five common but questionable principles of multimedia learning. In Mayer, R. (Ed.) Cambridge Handbook of Multimedia Learning. Cambridge University Press.

Cockbum, A. 1999. Teaching Mathematics with Insight. Palmer Press.

Coffield et al. 2004. Learning styles and pedagogy in post-16 learning.

Coles, R. 1989. The call of stories. Boston, MA: Houghton Mifflin.

Cowley, S. 2012. The Calm Classroom – 50 Techniques for Better Behaviour. Sue Cowley Books Ltd.

Compayré, G. 1886. The History of Pedagogy. Boston: D.C. Heath & Company.

Crooks, T. 2001. 'The validity of formative assessments', British Educational Research Association Conference. University of Leeds.

Darling-Hammond, L., Hammerness, K., Grossman, P., Rust, F. and Shulman, L. 2005. The design of teacher education programs. In Darling-Hammond, L. and Bransford, J. (eds.), Preparing teachers for a changing world: What teachers should learn and be able to do. San Francisco: Wiley, Ch. 10.

Derrington, C and Goddard, H. 2008. 'Whole-Brain' Behaviour Management in the Classroom. Routledge Taylor & Francis Group.

Dillon, J T. 1985. Using questions to foil discussion. Teaching and Teacher Education, 1 (2), pp. 109-121.

Dweck, C. S. 2006. Mindset – Changing the way you think to fulfil your potential. Robinson.

Eaude, T. 2006. Children's Spiritual, Moral, Social and Cultural

Development. Learning Matters Ltd.

EFHOH. European Federation of Hard of Hearing People. 2015. Hearing Loss – the Statistics. https://efhoh.org/wp-content/uploads/2017/04/Hearing-Loss-Statistics-AGM-2015.pdf

Emdin, C. 2017. Ted Talk: Teach teachers how to create magic.

https://www.ted.com/talks/christopher_emdin_teach_teachers_how_to_create_magic/discussion

Evans, R. 1996. The Human Side of School Change – Reform, Resistance, and the Real-life Problems of Innovation. Jossey-Bass Inc.

Fleming, J. 2013. Media Literacy, News Literacy, or News Appreciation? A Case Study of the News Literacy Program at Stony Brook University. Journalism & Mass Communication Educator. Glotzbach, R, Mohler, J and Radwan, J. 2009. Really Simple Syndication (RSS): An Educational Approach. Purdue University.

Fletcher-Wood, H. 2018. Responsive Teaching – Cognitive Science & Formative Assessment in Practice. A David Fulton Book

Fullan, M. and Stiegelbauer, S. 1991. The New Meaning of Educational Change. New York: Teachers College Press.

Gates, B. 2013. Ted Talk: Teachers need real feedback.

https://www.ted.com/talks/bill_gates_teachers_need_real_feedback

Geister, O. 2006. Große Kirchenordnung - Die Ordnung der Schule. Zur Grundlegung einer Kritik am verwalteten Unterricht. Münster.

Gershon, M. 2015. How to use Bloom's Taxonomy in the Classroom – The Complete Guide.

Gibson, R. 1998. Teaching Shakespeare: A Handbook for Teachers. Cambridge University Press.

Giles, M. 1990. Music and stress reduction in school children at risk for conduct disorders. Applications of Research in Music Education, 8(2), pp. 11-13.

Gray, P. 2008. A Brief History of Education. Psychology Today. Retrieved from https://www.psychologytoday.com/us/blog/freedom-learn/200808/brief-history-education

Grazak, E. 2013, November. Lessons from lunch detention. Education Week, 33(12). Retrieved from https://www.edweek.org/ew/articles/2013/11/13/12grazek.h33.html

Grendler, P. F. 2004. The universities of the Renaissance and Reformation. Renaissance Quarterly, 57.

Goldstein, S. and Brooks, B. 1995. Understanding & Managaing Children's Behavior. John Wiley & Sons, Inc.

Gupta, Amita. 2007. Going to School in South Asia. Greenwood Publishing Group.

Hallowell, E. M. 1994. Driven to Distraction. Recognizing and Coping with Attention Deficit Disorder from Childhood Through Adulthood. Touchstone.

Hamelink, C. 1976. An Alternative to News. Journal of Communication. Volume 26, Issue 4, pp. 120-123.

Hamilton, J. 2009. Journalism's Roving Eye: a history of American foreign reporting, Baton Rouge: Louisiana State University Press.

Hamre, B.K. and Pianta, R.C. 2005. Can instructional and emotional support in the first-grade classroom make a difference for children at risk of school failure? Child Development, 76(5), 949 – 967.

Hansen, A. 2005. Children's Errors in Mathematics. Learning Matters.

Hardiman, M. 2012. The Brain-Targeted Teaching Model for 21st Century Schools. Corwin.

Hardy, Grant & Kinney, Anne B. 2005. *The Establishment of the Han Empire and Imperial China*. Greenwood Publishing Group.

Hattie, J. 2012. Visible Learning for Teachers – Maximizing the Impact on Learning. Routledge Taylor & Francis Group.

Hattie, J. and Yates, G. 2013. Visible learning and the science of how we learn. Routledge Taylor & Francis Group.

Hattie, J. 2009. Visible Learning: A Synthesis of Over 800 Meta-Analyses Relating to Achievement. Routledge; 1 edition.

Hattie, J. 2015. What Works Best in Education: The Politics of Collaborative Expertise. Pearson. Retrieved from https://www.pearson.com/content/dam/one-dot-com/one-dot-com/global/standalone/hattie/files/150526_ExpertiseWEB_V1.pdf

Hattie, J. & Clarke, S. 2019. Visible Learning Feedback. Routledge.

Haylock, D. 1991. Teaching Mathematics to Low Attainers, 8-12. Paul Chapman Publishing Ltd.

Hawkes, N. 2013. From My Heart: Transforming Lives Through Values. Independent Thinking Press an imprint of Crown House Publishing.

Hembree, R., Experiments and relational studies in problem solving: a meta-analysis. Journal for Research in Mathematics Education, 1992. 23(3): pp. 242-273.

Hiebert, J., Gallimore, R, R., Garnier, H., Givvin, K. B., Hollingsworth, H., Jacobs, J. K., et al. 2003. Teaching mathematics in several countries: Results from the TIMSS 1999 video study (NCES No, 2003-013). Washington, DC: National Centre for education Statistics.

Hillman, C. H., Buck, S. L., Themanson, J. R., Pontifex, M. B., & Castelli, D. M. 2009. Aerobic fitness and cognitive development: Event-related brain potential and task performance indices of executive control in preadolescent children. Development Psychology, 45(1), pp. 114-129.

Hirsch, E.D., JR. 2017. Why Knowledge Matters – Rescuing Our Children from Failed Educational Theories. Harvard Education Press.

Hobbs, R. 1998. Building citizenship skills through media literacy education. In M. Salvador & P. Sias (Eds.), The public voice in a democracy at risk. Westport, CT: Praeger (pp. 57 –76).

Hobbs, Renee. 2004. A Review of School-Based Initiatives in Media Literacy Education. American Behavioral Scientist, Vol. 48, No. 1 (2004): 42-59. Print.

Hobbs, R. 2010. News Literacy: What Works and What Doesn't. University of Rhode Island. Student ID: 7125928 39 Kellner, D and Share, J. 2007. Critical Media Literacy Is Not an Option. Learning Inquiry 1, no. 1: 59–69. Hughes, M. 1986. Children and number: difficulties in learning mathematics. Oxford: Basil Blackwell.

Hughes, W. H. and Pickeral, T. 2013. School climate and shared leadership. In T. Dary and T. Pickeral (Ed.), School climate practices for implementation and sustainability. A School Climate Practice Brief, Number 1. New York: National School Climate Center.

Januszewski and M. Molenda (Eds.). 2008. Association for Educational Communications and Technology. Educational Technology: A definition with commentary. New York: Lawrence Erlbaum Associates.

Jennings, P & Siegel. 2015. Mindfulness for Teachers: Simple Skills for Peace and Productivity in the Classroom. 1st Edition. W. W. Norton & Company.

Karremans, J.C., Shellekens, M.P., & Kappen, G. 2017. Bridging the sciences of mindfulness and romantic relationships: a theoretical model and research agenda. Personality and Social Psychology Review, 21(1), 29-49.

Kell, E. 2018. How to Survive Teaching: Without imploding, exploding or walking away. Bloomsbury Education.

Kelley, K. 2016. The Inevitable – Understanding the Twelve Technological Forces that will Shape Our Future. Penguin Books.

Khwaja, C. 2006. The Role of Subject Knowledge in the Effective Teaching of Primary Science. ResearchGate.

Kingston, N. and Nash, B. 2011. Formative assessment: A meta-analysis and a call for research. Educational Measurement: Issuesand Practice, 30(4), pp. 28 – 37.

Kini, T. and Podolsky, A. 2016. Does teaching experience increase teacher effectiveness? A review of the research. Palo Alto: Learning Policy Institute.

Kok, B. E. & Singer, T. 2017. Effects of contemplative dyads on engagements and perceived social connectedness over 9 months of mental training: a randomized clinical trial. JAMA Psychiatry, 74(2), 126-134.

Kolb, D.A. 1984. Experiential Learning: Experience as the Source of Learning and Development

Kulik, J. A., & Kulik, C. L. C. 1992. Meta-analytic findings on grouping programs. Gifted Child Quarterly, 36(2), 73-77.

Laufenberg, Diana. Telephone interview. 28 May 2010. Quoted by Powers, 2010.

Laurillard, D. 2012. Teaching as a Design Science: Building Pedagogical Patterns for Learning and Technology. Routledge.

Leithwood, K. A. and Riehl, C. 2003. What we know about successful school leadership. Nottingham, England: National College for School Leadership.

Loughran, J., Berry, A. and Mulhall, P. 2012. Understanding and developing science teachers' pedagogical content knowledge: 2nd edition. Rotterdam: Sense Publishers.

Louv, R. Last Child in the Woods: Saving Our Children From Nature-Deficit Disorder. Algonquin Books.

Luckin. 2006. The learner centric ecology of resources: A framework for using technology to scaffold learning. Computers in Education. 50(2):449-462

MacBlain, S. 2014. How Children Learn. London: Sage.

Marrou, H. I. 1956. A History of Education in Antiquity. The University of Wisconsin Press.

McBride, D. M., & Dosher, A. B. 2002. A comparison of conscious and automatic memory processes for picture and word stimuli: A process dissociation analysis. Consciousness and Cognition, 11(3), 423-460.

McCann, S. 2017. Detention Is Not the Answer. Northwestern College, Iowa. NWCommons. Master's Theses & Capstone Projects – Education. https://nwcommons.nwciowa.edu/cgi/viewcontent.cgi?article=1069&cont ext=education_masters

McKeown, G. 2014. Essentialism: The Disciplined Pursuit of Less. Virgin Books.

McLuhan, M. 1964. Understanding Media: The Extensions of Man. 1st MIT Press edition.

McLuhan, M and Parker, H. 1969. Counterblast.

Mieke Van Houtte. 2004. Why boys achieve less at school than girls: the difference between boys' and girls' academic culture. Educational Studies 30 (2):159-173

Mihailidis, P. 2011. News Literacy. Global Perspectives for the Newsroom and Classroom.

Miller, A. 2007. Ted Talk: The News about the News.
http://www.ted.com/talks/alisa_miller_shares_the_news_about_the_news

Mishra and J. Koelher. 2006. Technological Pedagogical Content Knowledge: A Framework for Teacher Knowledge. Teachers College Record. 108:1017-1054.

Newport, C. 2016. Ted Talk: Why you should quit social media.

https://www.ted.com/talks/cal_newport_why_you_should_quit_social_media?language=en

Montessori, M. 1967. The absorbant mind. New York, NY: Henry Holt.

Nuthall, G. 2007. The hidden lives of learners, 1st ed. Wellington, NZ: New Zealand Council for Educational Research.

Olson, Sigurd. 1967. The Singing Wilderness. Knopf; 4th Printing edition.

Ornstein, A & Levine, D. 2004. Foundations of Education. 9th Edition. Wadsworth Publishing.

Orton, A., Frobisher, L. 1996. Insights into Teaching Mathematics. Cassell.

Palmer, S. 2009. 21st Century Boys: How modern life can drive them off the rails and how to get them back on track. Orion Books Ltd.

Palmer, B., Fletcher, H. and Shapley, B. 1994. Improving Student Reading, Writing with Newspaper-Based Instruction. Newspaper Research Journal 15, 50-55.

Pariser, E. The Filter Bubble: How the New Personalized Web Is Changing What We Read and How We Think. Penguin Press.

Patterson, Thomas E. "The Internet and the Threat It Poses to Local Media: Lessons from News in the Schools." Carnegie-Night Task Force on the Future of Journalism, 2007. Web. 17 July 2010.

Pedro De Bruyckere & Paul A. Kirschner. 2015. The myths of the digital native and the multitasker. Teaching and Teacher Education 67 (2017) 135e142

Peale, N. V. 1953. The Power of Positive Thinking – A Practical Guide to Mastering the Problems of Everyday Living. Prentice Hall.

Pearce, J. M. 2012. The case for open source appropriate technology. Environment, Development & Sustainability. Volume 14, Issue 3, pp 425–431.

Pekrun, R., Goetz, T., Titz, W., & Perry, R. P. 2002. Academic emotions in students' self-regulated learning and achievement: A program of qualitative and quantitative research. Educational Psychologist, 37(2), 91-105.

Peterson, P L; Carpenter, T & Fennema, E. 1989. Teachers knowledge of students' knowledge of mathematics problem solving: correlation and case analyses. Journal of Educational Psychology, 81(4), pp. 558-569.

Pierson, R. 2013. Ted Talk: Every Child Needs a Champion. https://www.ted.com/talks/rita_pierson_every_kid_needs_a_champion?re ferrer=playlist-tv_special_ted_talks_educatio#t-301411

Plevin, R. 2016. Take Control of the Noisy Class – From Chaos to Calm in 15 Seconds. Crown House Publishing.

Plutarch. 1927. Moralia (Volume 1). Cambridge, MA: Loeb Classical Library, Harvard University Press.

Powers, E. 2010. Teaching News Literacy in the Age of New Media: Why Secondary School Students Should Be Taught to Judge the Credibility of the News They Consume. Washington University in St. Louis.

Puentedura, R. 2015. SAMR Model. Technology is Learning. Retrieved from https://sites.google.com/a/msad60.org/technology-is-learning/samr-model

Ravitch, D. 2003. A Brief History of Teacher Professionalism. U.S. Department of Education. White House Conference on Preparing Tomorrow's Teachers.

https://www2.ed.gov/admins/tchrqual/learn/preparingteachersconference /ravitch.html

Recht, D. R. and Leslie, L. 1988. Effect of prior knowledge on good and poor readers' memory of text. Journal of Educational Psychology, 80, pp. 16 – 20.

Reese, S. D., & Lewis, S. 2009. Framing the War on Terror: Internalization of policy by the U.S. press. Journalism: Theory, Practice, Criticism.

Reese, S. 2012. Global News literacy: The Educator. Global News literacy: The Educator (Chapter prepared for News literacy: Global perspectives for the newsroom and the classroom). University of Texas at Austin.

Reichert, M & Hawley, R. 2010. Reaching Boys, Teaching Boys: Strategies that Work – and Why. Jossey Bass.

Riché, P. 1978. Education and Culture in the Barbarian West: From the Sixth through the Eighth Century. Columbia: University of South Carolina Press.

Roberts, J. M. & Westad, Odd Arne. 2013. The Penguin History of the World (Sixth edition). New York: Penguin Books.

Rohrer, D & Pshler, H. 2012. Learning styles: where's the evidence? Medical education. Volume 46, Issue 7. Blackwell Publishing Ltd.

Ruttle, P. L., Shirtcliff, E. A., Serbin, L. A., Ben-Dat Fisher, D., Stack, D. M., & Schwartzman, A. E. 2011. Disentangling psychobiological mechanisms underlying internalizing and externalizing behaviors in youth: Longitudinal and concurrent associations with cortisol. Hormones and Behavior, 59(1), 123-132.

Schwarz, G & Brown, P. 2006. Media Literacy: Transforming Curriculum and teaching. Oklahoma State University: Wiley-Blackwell.

Schwarz, F. 2010. Media Literacy and the News. Windesheim School of Media in Zwolle, the Netherlands.

Schwartz, S. 2012. An Overview of the Schwartz Theory of Basic Values. Conceptual Issues in Psychology and Culture. Retrieved from https://scholarworks.gvsu.edu/cgi/viewcontent.cgi?article=1116&context=orpc

Sheninger, E.C. 2016. Uncommon Leaning – Creating Schools That Work for Kids. Sage Publications Ltd.

Shepard, R. N. 1967. Recognition memory for words, sentences, and pictures. Journal of Verbal Learning and Verbal Behavior, 6(1), 156-163.

Sherman, S. and Frea, A. 2004. The Wild West of executive coaching. Harvard Business Review, 82(11), 82-90.

Shonkoff, J. P., & Phillips, D. 2000. From neurons to neighborhoods: The science of early childhood development. Washington, DC: National Academy Press.

Schumacher, E. F. 1973. Small is Beautiful. Bond & Briggs Ltd. London.

Shuard, H., Walsh, A., Goodwin, J. and Worcester, V. 1990. Children, Mathematics and Learning. Simon & Schuster.

Silverman, F. H. 1988. The "Monster" Study. Marquette University.

Simmons, A. 2013. I Am a Teacher With Really Bad Handwriting. The Atlantic. Education Article. Retrieved from https://www.theatlantic.com/education/archive/2013/12/i-am-a-teacher-with-really-bad-handwriting/282379/

Slater, H., Davies, N. and Burgess, S. 2012. Do teachers matter? Measuring the variation in teacher effectiveness in England. Oxford Bulletin of Economics and Statistics, 74, 629 – 645.

Smith, T & Butcher, T. 2007. Essential Reporting: The NCTJ Guide for Trainee Journalists. Sage Publications.

Smyth, V. 1979. Speech reception in the presence of classroom noise. Language, Speech, and Hearing Services in Schools, 10(4), pp. 221-230.

Snowden, D. 2003. The Nun Study. Information retrieved from the official website. https://web.archive.org/web/20131229163933/https://www.healthstudies.umn.edu/nunstudy/

Soysal, Y N & Strang, D. 1989. Construction of the First Mass Education Systems in Nineteenth-Century Europe. Sociology of Education. 62 (4): 277-288.

Stagg, L. 2013. International Mindedness: Global Perspectives for Learners and Educators. Urban Publications Ltd.

Street, B., Baker, D., Tomlin, A. 2005. Navigating Numeracies. Springer.

Thomas, G. 2013. Education – A Very Short Introduction. Oxford University Press.

Thomason, Allison Karmel. 2005. Luxury and Legitimation: Royal Collecting in Ancient Mesopotamia. Ashgate Publishing, Ltd.

Timimi, Sami. 2005. Naughty Boys: anti-social behavior, ADHD and the role of culture. Palgrave Macmillan.

TokJn, K. 1986. Effects of teacher wait time on discourse characteristics in mathematics and art classes. American Educational Research Journal, 23(2), pp. 191-200.

Tomlinson, C., & McTighe, J. 2006. Integrating differentiated instruction & understanding by design: Connecting content and kids. Alexandria, VA: Association for Supervision and Curriculum Development.

Tuckman, B. W. 1965. Developmental sequence in small groups. *Psychological Bulletin, 63*(6), 384-399.

Tudor, M. 1939. An experimental study of the effect of evaluative labeling on speech fluency. Master's thesis, University of Iowa.

Vaill, P. B. 1989. Managing as a Performing Art: New Ideas for a World of Chaotic Change. San Francisco: Jossey-Bass.

Van Houtte, M. 2004. Why boys achieve less at school than girls: the difference between boys' and girls' academic culture. Educational Studies, Vol. 30, No. 2, June 2004. Ghent University, Belgium.

Voss, C. and Raz, T. 2016. Never Split the Difference: Negotiating As If Your Life Depended On It. HarperCollins Publishers.

Way, J. and Beardon, T. 2003. ICT as a Tool for Learning – Where are we going?', in Way, J. and Beardon, T. (Eds.) ICT and Primary Mathematics. OU Press.

Webb, N. M. 1991. Task-related verbal interaction and mathematics learning in small groups. Journal for Research in Mathematics Education, 22(5): pp. 366-389.

Wentzel, K. R., & Wigfield, A. 1998. Academic and social motivational influences on student's academic performance. Educational Psychology Review, 10(2), 155-175.

Whitworth, A. 2009. Information Obesity. Chandos, Oxford, UK.

Wiliam, D. 2016. Leadership for teacher learning: Creating a culture where all teachers improve so that all students succeed. West Palm Beach, FL: Learning Sciences International.

Wiliam, D. 2018. Embedded Formative Assessment. Solution Tree Press.

Williams KA, Kolar MM, Reger BE, Pearson JC. 2001. Evaluation of a wellness-based mindfulness stress reduction intervention: A controlled trial. American Journal of Health Promotion. 15: 422–432.

Williams, M & Penman, D. 2011. Mindfulness: A Practical Guide to Finding Peace in a Frantic World. Piatkus.

Willingham, D.T. 2009. Why Don't Students Like School? San Francisco: Jossey-Bass.

Woodward, H. 2000. Portfolios: Narratives for learning. Journal of In-Service Education Vol 26 No 2 p. 329 -347.

Zander, B. 2008. Ted Talk: The Transformative Power of Classical Music.

https://www.ted.com/talks/benjamin_zander_on_music_and_passion

Zuckerman, E. 2010. Ted Talk: Listening to Global Voices.
http://www.youtube.com/watch?v=vXPJVwwEmiM

Printed in Great Britain
by Amazon

34950222R00142